Elizabeth R
A PHOTOGRAPHIC CELEBRATION
OF 40 YEARS

Elizabeth R

A PHOTOGRAPHIC CELEBRATION
OF 40 YEARS

SELECTED BY
LORD LICHFIELD

DOUBLEDAY

LONDON – NEW YORK – TORONTO – SYDNEY – AUCKLAND

Frontispiece: The Queen in the Irish State Coach,
leaving Buckingham Palace for the State
Opening of Parliament in November 1971.
Amidst all the pomp and pageantry I managed
to snap this light-hearted moment.

Title page: In the first formal portrait study taken after her
accession the Queen is wearing a black taffeta gown and the
diamond necklace given to her as a wedding present by the
Nizam of Hyderabad. Photo by Dorothy Wilding in May 1952.

© Berkswell Publishing Co Ltd 1991
Produced by John Stidolph
Edited by Charles Jacoby
Assistant designer Sally Alexander

First published in 1991 by DOUBLEDAY
a division of Transworld Publishers Ltd
61–63 Uxbridge Road, London W5 5SA

DOUBLEDAY, a division of Bantam Doubleday Dell
Publishing Group Inc. 666 Fifth Avenue,
New York, New York 10103.

DOUBLEDAY CANADA LTD
105 Bond Street, Toronto, Ontario

TRANSWORLD PUBLISHERS (AUSTRALIA) PTY LTD
15–23 Helles Avenue, Moorebank, NSW 2170

TRANSWORLD PUBLISHERS (NZ) LTD
Cnr Moselle and Waipareira Aves, Henderson, Auckland

British Library Cataloguing in Publication Data applied for

ISBN 0 385 40266X

Typeset by Footnote Graphics, Warminster
Originated and printed in Hong Kong
Produced by Mandarin Offset Ltd.

CONTENTS

This is one of my favourite pictures. I shot it at Balmoral in 1972 when I was taking pictures for the Queen's Silver Wedding celebrations. It was achieved without a reflector or an assistant, with me kneeling uncomfortably on the grass by a loch. It proves firstly that a photographer's greatest asset is luck. I used only one roll of film, as the light was fading, and yet managed to get two or three pictures good enough to be distributed worldwide and even used on a stamp in Australia. The Queen and the Duke of Edinburgh are wonderful subjects. The relaxed and happy expressions show what professionals they are at their jobs.

PREFACE

Lord Mountbatten used to say that Her Majesty the Queen possesses a quality impossible to capture on film; and hence, no photograph could ever do her justice. I know exactly what he meant, but I take a slightly different view because, although it is not possible to capture the full range of her character in a single photograph, I believe that a well chosen selection of pictures is able to convey something of the wisdom and strength of her personality as well as the incredible breadth of experience she has acquired.

None the less, when I was asked to choose the pictures for this book, I had to explain to the publishers that it would be an invidious task to select just 150 pictures of the most photographed person in the world, taken over a period of almost half a century.

So we decided to start the search in the archives of Camera Press, the world famous agency founded by the late Tom Blau, which handles the work of many famous photographers, including most of those who have been commissioned to take official portraits. But we decided that to offset the formality of portraits, we needed the informality of photojournalism to show the background changes that have occurred during the Queen's reign.

I was involved in launching the annual Martini Royal Photographic Competition almost twenty years ago. It has consistently produced the very best in photojournalism and we have been able to augment our selection of portraits with some less formal pictures from the competition and also with archive material from the press agencies. Of course it has been painful to leave out a great many brilliant photographs, but in the end we have come up with a selection which I think reflects and celebrates forty years of the Queen's reign, and I hope conveys something of the indefinable quality to which Lord Mountbatten referred.

1952–1962

'THE TRADITION OF MY FAMILY'

'It is my resolve that under God I shall not only rule but serve. That is not only the tradition of my family; it describes, I believe, the modern character of the British Crown.'
The Queen, at the opening of the Australian Parliament, February 1954.

I have chosen the picture of the coronation opposite, not only to sum up the responsibilities the Queen acceded to in 1952, but also to show the load she bears to this day. In the picture she is a diminutive figure weighed by the trappings of state in the nave of the spiritual centre of the British Commonwealth, Westminster Abbey, under remorseless chandeliers. The Queen, flanked by maids of honour, processes down the aisle after the service on the 2nd June 1953. The remorselessness of the glare of public enquiry has diminished not one jot, yet throughout her reign the Queen has hardly put a foot wrong.

On the night of the 5th February 1952, King George VI died at Sandringham aged 56. He had been shooting hares on that crisp February day, but by the morning of the 6th, when his valet brought his tea, the King's life had slipped away. The doctors diagnosed a heart attack. The new Queen did not learn of her accession until some hours after most people in Britain. She was with the Duke of Edinburgh and her lady-in-waiting, Lady Pamela Mountbatten, daughter of Lord Mountbatten, in Kenya. The people of Kenya had given Princess Elizabeth a hunting lodge in the Aberdare Forest Game Reserve as a wedding present. She was staying at the nearby Treetops Hotel when the news reached Nairobi by wire from the press agency Reuters. It was passed by a journalist to her secretary of three years, Major the Hon. Martin Charteris. At 11.45 a.m. GMT he telephoned Prince Philip's private secretary Michael Parker. He, in turn, informed the Prince who walked over to the new Queen, took her aside, and the two walked alone for some time on the banks of the Sagana River. All further engagements in Kenya were cancelled and plans were made for an immediate return to England.

In London the Prime Minister, Winston Churchill, was worried for the future. 'I don't know her,' he said to his private secretary Jock Colville. 'She's a mere child. I knew the King so well.' 'You will find her the reverse of being a child,' replied Colville, who had been her private secretary for two years before Charteris. Colville was to be proved right. 'I, whose youth was passed in the august, unchallenged and tranquil glare of the Victorian era, may well feel a thrill in invoking once more the prayer and the anthem "God Save the Queen",' declared Churchill later.

As a normal precaution the Queen's baggage had been packed with mourning clothes and documents of inheritance. She signed the papers and put on the clothes (and with those clothes a distinctive attitude of queenship) to fly from Entebbe to London. Telegrams were sent to Australia and New Zealand, countries she was due to visit, apologising for her enforced absence. Presents and mementoes were given as normal to the staff at the game reserve. 'What name will you use as sovereign?' she was asked; after all her father had been christened Albert, and monarchs frequently take names other than those by which they are known. 'Oh my own name – what else?' she said, a little dazedly.

She was met at the airport by Attlee, Churchill and Eden, prime ministers past, present and to come. Her uncle, the Duke of Gloucester was there too. In Clarence House, at 4 o'clock in the afternoon on the day after the King's death, Queen Mary announced, 'Her old granny and subject must be the first to kiss her hand.' George VI was the third son the old Queen had seen laid to rest.

The remainder of the month of February was filled with affairs of state for the twenty-five year-old new Queen. At the accession council many of her privy councillors were wearing well-worn, ration-book clothes. The lying-in-state of the King took place in Westminster Hall. The Queen received high commissioners, Commonwealth representatives and members of foreign royal families. The funeral took place in St George's Chapel, Windsor. Afterwards the Queen held her first investiture and approved the wording of prayers for the royal family. She was proclaimed Queen Elizabeth II.

By June she was living in Buckingham Palace, and court mourning ended. She held her first official Birthday Parade, the Trooping the Colour, and presided over her coronation council. Her coronation was proclaimed for 2nd June the following year.

Her mother, Queen Elizabeth, endured a period of great private grief after the funeral of her husband. However, she too had duties to perform. The Duke of Edinburgh once said that the monarch has to 'live above the shop,' and so it was that Queen Elizabeth moved out of Buckingham Palace for the Queen, her daughter, to move in. In August 1952 she bought Barrowgill Castle in Caithness, in the northern highlands of Scotland. It was a place which would not remind her too much of her happy days with her husband yet where she could cherish his memory.

The Duke of Windsor visited Queen Mary in November 1952 for what was to be the last time. She died at Marlborough House on the 24th March 1953. At the end of that month she was laid to rest in St George's Chapel, Windsor, in the family vault. As she had stipulated in her will, there was to be no official mourning to interrupt the coronation.

The Queen was crowned on 2nd June 1953. It was a date chosen because the meteorological office deemed it sufficiently unlikely to rain. It poured. The event was televised and over twenty million people watched it live, while another twelve million heard it on the wireless. For the inestimable effect that the coronation had on the nation, Malcolm Muggeridge suggested that BBC commentator Richard Dimbleby should be awarded the title 'Gold Microphone in Waiting'.

The Queen devoted her first decade on the throne above all to the establishment of the Commonwealth. The British Empire had come to an end, and the last of a mixed portfolio of countries were planning or actively accepting independence. Cynics say the Commonwealth is Britain hopelessly clinging to an empire it has lost. But most commentators affirm that it is a unique association of nations linked by a common allegiance to the Queen. She made it her mission to bind this association. The film of her coronation permeated most nooks and corners of the red bits on the map on my schoolroom wall.

In November 1953 the Queen and the Duke of Edinburgh set off to circumnavigate the world. She was the first reigning monarch to do so. In her own words: 'The strongest bonds of all are those which are recorded not in documents but in the hearts of the people who share the same beliefs and the same aims.' Churchill, who by now had said those famous words about his sovereign: 'What a very attractive and intelligent young woman,' pronounced of the first grand tour, 'It may well be that the journey the Queen is about to take will be no less auspicious and the treasure she brings back no less bright than when Drake first sailed an English ship around the world.'

It was a damp late autumn evening when she left the country. Bermuda was considerably sunnier, and from there the royal party set course for Jamaica. The Shaw Savill liner *Gothic* carried them through the Panama Canal to Fiji and to Tonga where the colourful Queen Selote was waiting with a London taxicab which she had bought on her visit to England for the coronation.

Godfrey Talbot, the veteran royal commentator, was travelling with the party, and he recalled for me the fun and laughter which accompanied the trip. It was as *Gothic* was making a spectacular arrival in port that Godfrey made his classic spoonerism on air describing the splendour of the scene as 'the Royal Clot, *Yothic*, floats serenely above all the other craft'.

The royal party went on to New Zealand from where the Queen made her Christmas broadcast to the Commonwealth. She spent a month in Australia where she rested for a total of six days on a tour which included travelling nearly 14,000 miles, making over 100 speeches and listening to twice that number. The next leg of the trip took her to Uganda via the Cocos Islands, Ceylon and Aden. Pamela Mountbatten was with her again and they were met by Lord Mountbatten in Libya, and reunited with Prince Charles and Princess Anne who had been staying with him in Malta. It was there also that the Queen took possession of her new Royal Yacht *Britannia*. This imposing vessel has become closely identified with her tours around the world, and is suitably magnificent. They sailed home by way of Gibraltar, to receive a welcome, as they steamed up the Thames, the like of which has not been seen since.

The Queen's state visits during the rest of the decade included Norway in June 1955, Nigeria in January 1956, Sweden in June 1956, Portugal in February 1957, France in April, Denmark in May, Canada and the USA in October 1957 and the Netherlands in March 1958. In 1959 she returned to Canada and the USA and in 1961 having rested for six months after the birth of Prince Andrew, she and Prince Philip visited Cyprus, India, Pakistan, Nepal and Turkey. Later that year they went to Italy and the Vatican where they met Pope John XXIII, and they undertook a gruelling tour of the countries of West Africa. Travel in the 1950s was much slower than it is today, so by any standards that was an impressive schedule.

Heads of state who were received by the Queen in London included Haile Selassie of Ethiopia, Nehru of India, Tito of Yugoslavia, Cravero Lopes of Portugal, Bulganin and Kruschev of the USSR, who met her at Windsor Castle, King Feisal of Iraq and the Shahanshah of Iran, Gronchi of Italy and Heuss of West Germany. Then in 1960 General de Gaulle came, followed by the President of Pakistan and President Frondizi of Argentina. President John F Kennedy came to supper in 1961. President Tubman of Liberia came in 1962, but President Soekarno of Indonesia decided he could not leave Jakarta and cancelled his proposed visit to London.

On the family side of her life there was the distress over Princess Margaret's desire to, and final decision not to, marry the dashing Group Captain Peter Townsend. That episode, perhaps more than any other, brought the Queen closer to her sister. In any large family there are bound to be occasions of joy at the births and marriages of relations, and sadness at the deaths of others. I have already mentioned the deaths of the Queen's father and grandmother, and in December 1956 Princess Marie-Louise died aged 84. The following month Queen Mary's brother, the Earl of Athlone, died aged 82, so the winter of 1956/57 was not a particularly happy one.

Prince Charles and Princess Anne were growing up, giving great delight to their parents. In 1960 Prince Andrew was born, and the same month Princess Margaret announced her engagement to my fellow photographer Tony Armstrong-Jones. They were married in May of that year and the following year the Duke of Kent married Katharine Worsley at York Minster. Lo and behold, a year later the Duke's sister Princess Alexandra was engaged to Angus Ogilvy and we had three royal weddings in as many years. They had the effect of bringing the royal family onto television and making them easily recognisable by the public.

Although she was determined to be a modern monarch, the internal workings of Buckingham Palace held the Queen back. The 1950s were the stuffiest days of her reign. Prince Philip was a useful broom and some of the cobwebs were swept out. New blood was introduced to the court; but it took criticism from Lord Altrincham and a subsequent public debate before the Palace mandarins allowed real change to take place, and that was not to be until the next decade.

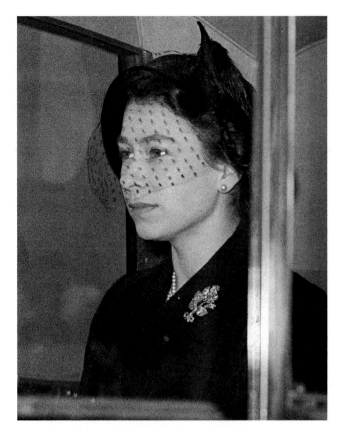

The Queen on the morning of 25th March 1953, arriving at Marlborough House. Queen Mary died there peacefully in her sleep at 10.20 p.m. the night before, aged 85. Her friend Lady Airlie remembers going to visit the old Queen a few months before when she was in bed with a cold: 'It was a dull grey November day when I entered the familiar door at Marlborough House. I was taken straight to her bedroom and having been warned not to make her talk on account of the cough which was troubling her, I chatted away about trivial things. All the while I was conscious of everything around her: the exquisitely soft lawn nightgown – the same as those worn in her youth – the nails delicately shaped and polished a pale pink; the immaculately arranged grey hair. Her face had still a gentle beauty of expression; no trace of hardness as so many faces have in old age, only resignation. As I kissed her hand before leaving I noticed the extreme softness of her skin, I went back to Airlie happier for having seen her, not knowing it was for the last time.'

I love this picture, it is such a famous image, and contrasts extraordinarily well with the picture beside it. It is a close-up of the newly crowned Queen wearing the Imperial State Crown, her sunny smile defying the grey weather, during her processional drive after her coronation. Although she had been crowned with St Edward's Crown in Westminster Abbey, she exchanged it for the lighter and more comfortable Imperial State Crown for the journey back to Buckingham Palace. However even that is quite a weight and imposes a considerable burden on its wearer.

These pictures depict the scene in Westminster Abbey during the coronation ceremony, just after the Queen was crowned. The expressions say everything. There is a mixture of solemnity and total awe on every face. In the gallery, top left, where most of the royal family sat, you can just see Prince William of Gloucester, his mother the Duchess and his brother Prince Richard, the present Duke. Below them stand the Duchess Dowager of Devonshire, Mistress of the Robes, and the Queen's six Maids-of-Honour, Lady Rosemary Spencer-Churchill, Lady Moyra Hamilton, Lady Jane Heathcote-Drummond-Willoughby, Lady Anne Coke, Lady Mary Baillie-Hamilton, and Lady Jane Vane-Tempest-Stewart. Gentleman Usher of the Black Rod General Sir Brian Horrocks stands next to them, and then Field-Marshal the Earl Alexander of Tunis who carried the Orb. Garter King of Arms, Sir George Bellew, heads a knot of heralds, and behind them, in the murk, are the various pages who included my old friend the Hon. Brian Alexander who was attending his father. The

morass with the coronets and robes are the peers, and three Princes of the Blood Royal stand in front of them, the Dukes of Edinburgh, Gloucester and Kent. On the left and right of the Queen stand the Bishop of Bath & Wells, the Right Reverend Harold Bradfield, and the Bishop of Durham, the Right Reverend Michael Ramsay, who later became Archbishop of Canterbury. On Ramsay's right is the Marquess of Salisbury who bore the Sword of State, but by then had exchanged it for a lighter model, and his opposite number on the other side of the throne, with his back to the camera, is the Lord Great Chamberlain, the Marquess of Cholmondeley. Facing the Queen is the Archbishop of Canterbury, the Most Reverend Geoffrey Fisher.

Above: The Queen processes through the streets of London after the coronation in Sir William Chambers' roccoco Gold State Coach. Chambers was clerk of works at the Royal Mews when in 1762 the Gold State Coach was delivered. It was hailed at the time as 'the most superb and expensive of any built in this kingdom'. Eight carved palm trees form the framework of the body and they hold up the roof. Those at each corner appear to grow from lions' heads, and they bear the fruits which symbolize British victories during the Seven Years War which had just finished. The 24-foot coach was regilded all over for the event. Its panels, front and back, were painted by the Italian artist Giovanni Battista Cipriani. It has been drawn by eight horses in red Moroccan leather harness for all the coronations since George IV. In days of yore it was used at the Opening of Parliament too.

The family photograph after the coronation ceremony in Buckingham Palace. From left to right they are: Princess Alexandra of Kent, Prince Michael of Kent, Princess Marina the Duchess of Kent, Princess Margaret, the Duke of Gloucester, the Queen, the Duke of Edinburgh, Queen Elizabeth the Queen Mother, the Duke of Kent, the Princess Royal, the Duchess of Gloucester, Prince William of Gloucester, and Prince Richard of Gloucester. At the service itself the Archbishop of Canterbury prayed that the Queen might receive 'the spirit of wisdom and government, the spirit of counsel and ghostly strength, the spirit of knowledge and true godliness'. In the last forty years she has added to this list the spirit of experience. With tours across most of the world's surface and millions of airmiles on the clock she is in the highest echelons of the world's most travelled people.

Queen Elizabeth and the Duke of Edinburgh receive the
acclaim of the nation and the Commonwealth on the
balcony of Buckingham Palace after the coronation
ceremony. She has a freshness in her face which begged
the question at the time, is she too young to rule? The
answer was emphatically not. Everyone near her on that
fateful day sixteen months before noticed the change
which swept over her.

This is the most important picture Beaton ever took of the Queen. It is an astonishing, highly technical, filmic photograph and an extraordinary light job. In a sense it is an icon. She wears the coronation robes as she sits in front of a painted backdrop of Henry VII's Chapel, Westminster Abbey, which Beaton erected in the Green Drawing Room at Buckingham Palace. She is wearing the Imperial State Crown and carries the orb and sceptre.

This, by Beaton again, is the poor relation of the picture opposite. It lacks that one's vulnerability, perhaps because of the presence of the Duke of Edinburgh. The Queen's white satin robes were designed by Norman Hartnell. The theme was floral emblems and included the standard rose for England, shamrock for Ireland, thistle for Scotland and leek for Wales as well as the lotus flower for Ceylon and protea for South Africa.

The Queen stands with Commonwealth prime ministers on 1st June 1953, the day before the coronation, when they had lunch at Buckingham Palace. Today the Commonwealth consists of some forty-nine members. They embrace a colourful cross-section of world culture from Tuvalu in the South Pacific which boasts a population of 8,000, to India, a sub-continent inhabited by 750 million. Most of these countries are republics with their own heads of state, but the Queen is actually Queen of Antigua and Barbuda, Australia, the Bahamas, Barbados, Belize, Canada, Fiji, Grenada, Jamaica, Mauritius, New Zealand, Papua New Guinea, St Christopher and Nevis, St Lucia, St Vincent and the Grenadines, the Solomon Islands, Tuvalu, and the United Kingdom of England, Scotland, Wales and Northern Ireland.

Left to right: Mohammed Ali of Pakistan, Sir Godfrey Huggins of Rhodesia, Lord Brookeborough of Northern Ireland, F G Holland of New Zealand, Pandit Nehru of India, Chief Minister of Jamaica Sir Alexander Bustamente, British Prime Minister Sir Winston Churchill, the Queen, Sir Robert Menzies of Australia, L S St Laurent of Canada, P S Senanayaka of Ceylon, Dr Malan of the Union of South Africa, and Dr Borg Oliver of Malta.

President of Yugoslavia Marshal Tito, with Queen
Elizabeth the Queen Mother, The Queen, the Duke of
Edinburgh and Princess Margaret, standing for the press
on the occasion of Tito's state visit in 1953. To govern a
country made up of at least six races speaking different
languages, the Serbs, the Croats, the Slovenes, the
Albanians, the Macedonians and the Yugoslavs, required
a political adroitness and ruthlessness second to none.
Tito abolished his country's monarchy in 1945.
Yugoslavia was then a fairly new country, made up of
the kingdoms of Serbia, Croatia, Bosnia and
Montenegro soon after the Great War. Peter II was the
country's second and last king, but he was the tenth
member of the Karageorgevich and Obrenovich
dynasties to rule. Tito was the only leader capable of
holding the country together, and now it seems to be
disintegrating.

The pictures on this page and opposite were all taken in 1953 by the famous royal photographer Baron, who was the Duke of Edinburgh's protégé, and Cecil Beaton's great rival. Baron Nahum, shortened always to Baron, was the son of a Jewish immigrant from Tripoli. He was brought up in Manchester, and went on to become a society photographer. His break came in 1935 whilst he was in the Army in Malta, when he met Lord Mountbatten who introduced him to the royal family. He became a personal friend of the Duke of Edinburgh and together they were members of the notorious all-male Thursday Club, which met at Wheelers restaurant in Soho, where lunch each week would go on into the evening. It was there that Baron organized an unofficial stag party for his patron a few days before his wedding to Princess Elizabeth at which Baron took the official pictures. He had a certain feel, much less theatrical than Beaton, more purist even, but to the layman less recognizable. There was enormous competition between them over who was to be commissioned to take the coronation pictures, and Beaton finally won, thanks to the influence of Queen Elizabeth the Queen Mother. However Beaton commented at the time that the 'Duke of E adopted a rather ragging attitude towards the proceedings. He would have preferred his friend Baron to take the pictures'. Baron was given his chance later in the year and might have become a much more serious threat to Beaton if he had not died unexpectedly in 1956. He had recently become engaged to be married to the beautiful and popular actress Sally-Anne Howes.

When sweating through a photographic session in the tropics, weighed down with camera gear, all photographers are thankful for shade. It also softens the harsh tropical light so obvious in these pictures. In the one above Queen Selote of Tonga sits between the Queen and the Duke of Edinburgh in December 1953 during a feast which consisted of no less than 2,000 pigs, duck, fish, lobster, crab, pineapple, yams, water melon, bananas and coconut, and which lasted most of the evening. The Queen tries to avoid seafood on foreign tours. The midday sun in Tonga can have a dire effect on a lobster. The Queen's visit to Tonga, the first ever by a reigning monarch, ended with her spending a day taking photographs of Polynesian scenes while the Duke of Edinburgh went swimming. According to the official record of the visit the Queen was 'both relaxed and happy in the presence of the exotic delights that only the charm of Queen Selote can diffuse'.

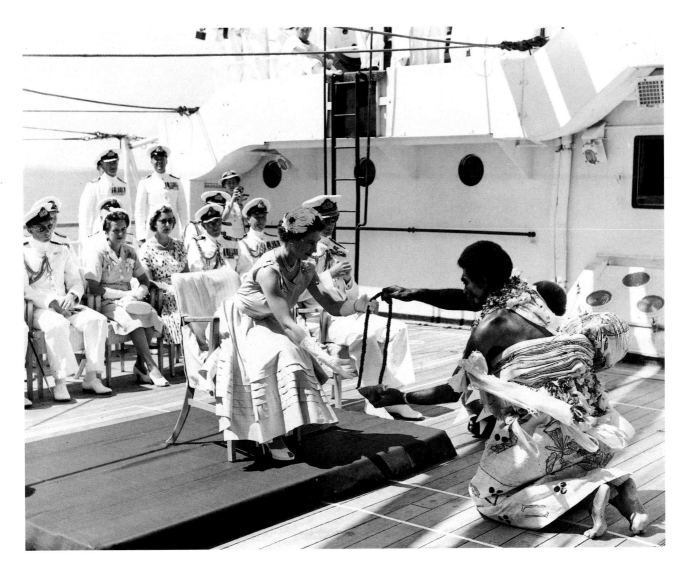

During the Queen's tour of the Pacific, *Gothic* hove into sight of the delightful islands of Fiji. In this picture a Fijian chief performs the traditional Invitation to Land ceremony on board *Gothic* in Suva Bay. He presented the Queen with the *tabua*, a necklace of whales' teeth, which is the Fijian formal disembarkation procedure. At a feast that evening the Queen bravely drank a cup of the fiery local brew *yaqona*, which in other islands is called *kava*, out of a coconut shell. She also went to a state ball where the official record states she was 'escorted by 200 glistening torch-bearers'. Among the people she met on the island was one John Christian, a descendant of the *Bounty* mutineer Fletcher Christian. Finally, she went on a tour of the islands by flying boat. There are some 840 islands in the archipelago but only 100 are inhabited. They lie in an area roughly 300 miles square. Both Fiji and Tonga became independent in 1970.

The Queen and the Duke of Edinburgh drove through
lines of hundreds of New Zealand schoolchildren
assembled at Pukekura Park in New Plymouth when
they arrived for a civic reception. On Christmas Day,
after a meal of turkey and plum pudding flown out from
London, she made a speech which crackled out on
crystal sets all over the Commonwealth: 'As I travel
across the world today I am ever more deeply impressed
with the achievement which the modern Commonwealth
presents. Like New Zealand, from whose North Island I
am speaking, everyone of its nations can be justly proud
of what it has built for itself on its own soil. But their
greatest achievement I suggest is the Commonwealth
itself, and that owes much to all of them.'

The interest in this photograph lies in the varying
heights of the subjects. Here the Queen, 5′ 2″, reviews
naval ratings from Papua New Guinea outside
Government House in Canberra on 15th February 1954.
She had arrived in Australia on 3rd February, the first
reigning monarch to do so. Australia welcomed her
warmly from the start. The illuminations and official
festivities cost the Sydney corporation some £2 million.
One of the highlights was the surf carnival at Bondi
Beach. In Canberra she opened the Australian
Parliament wearing her coronation robes which had been
specially shipped out. And then at Melbourne Cricket
Ground she was cheered by some 17,000 children. Later
in Queensland one of the children tried to kiss the
Queen. It came as a surprise to her but she managed to
disentangle herself tactfully from the four year-old girl.

The Queen, the Duke of Edinburgh, Prince Charles and
Princess Anne stand on the balcony of Buckingham
Palace in 1954 at the end of the world tour, receiving
the cheers of the crowds assembled in front of them.
Hundreds of Londoners had lined the banks of the
Thames as the brand new *Britannia* steamed up it.
Tower Bridge sported the words 'WELCOME HOME'
in huge letters. The Queen Mother and Princess
Margaret joined them at the Pool of London to go by
barge to Westminster Pier where other members of the
royal family greeted them. Meanwhile, on that short
voyage back from Malta the Queen had time to look at
her new yacht. As she had said at its launch: 'My father
felt most strongly, as I do, that a yacht was a necessity
and not a luxury for the head of our great
Commonwealth, between whose countries the sea is no
barrier, but the natural and indestructible highway.'

The Queen and the Duke of Edinburgh welcome King
Gustav VI Adolf of Sweden and Queen Louise to
Buckingham Palace on 28th June 1954. Queen Louise,
the Swedish King's second wife, was born a
Mountbatten. His first wife was Princess Margaret of
Connaught. He died in 1973 and was succeeded by his
grandson King Carl XVI Gustav whose father died
tragically in an aeroplane crash in 1947. The old King
was keen to train his grandson for the job in his
declining years. The Crown Prince was sent abroad to
learn about foreign affairs and spent time working for
the Swedish Embassy in London and for Hambros
bank. He also studied hard the subjects of Swedish
industry, business and agriculture. King Gustav Adolf's
daughter Ingrid married King Frederik IX of Denmark
pictured later in this chapter.

This portrait by Cecil Beaton was taken in the Ballroom at Buckingham Palace in 1955 for the Queen's three week tour of Nigeria. It is what Beaton was best at, but that chair is an odd frame for the picture. The crown almost disappears into the coat of arms at the top. I think he was being a little blasé. He noted at the time that it was difficult to find a new corner of the Palace to photograph the Queen in. 'By now I have taken so many sittings here and have somewhat exploited all the possibilities,' he said.

Opposite: This portrait by Baron from 1956 is a real pudding and pie picture of its era. Note the retouched colour of her arms, which seems to have been an attempt to put sleeves on, as well as the background which does not even come down to the floor! But it is brave to show the Queen against a plain grey background. It is in the style of the American photographer Irving Penn, whose work for *Vogue* especially I have long admired. Penn was the man who damned my smoking in his studio with the words 'One more cigarette like that and I'll have to adjust my exposure by a sixteenth of a stop'.

The Queen is welcomed to 10 Downing Street by Lady Churchill on the eve of Sir Winston's retirement as Prime Minister in April 1955. When Churchill resigned he did not raise the question of who was to be his successor with the Queen. He made it quite clear that that was not his position unless he was specifically asked. As it was, the answer was obvious to everyone. Anthony Eden was the choice. When Eden resigned in 1957 the choice between Harold Macmillan and R A Butler was more difficult, so the Queen asked Lord Salisbury and the Lord Chancellor to conduct a poll in Cabinet and report to her the answer while she asked for opinions from Winston Churchill, Lord Waverley and Lord Chandos. However, at the end of Macmillan's premiership in 1963 she did ask for his personal feelings about who should succeed him, and acting on it sent for Sir Alec Douglas-Home.

The Queen and the Duke of Edinburgh touched down in Lagos on Saturday 28th January 1956 to begin a three-week tour of Nigeria. Photographically speaking this tour suffered from the large amounts of red dust which settled on all equipment and proved impossible to wipe off. Here the Queen is seen receiving an address of welcome from the Oba of Lagos, Deniji Adele II, during a ceremony at the Lagos town boundary shortly after her arrival. There is a great deal of interest to be had from seeing how the white colonial rulers sit stony-faced at one end of the dais, while the Nigerians sit at the other end. Later in this book you can see how much more relaxed and integrated such gatherings have become. Another gulf the Queen bridged on that visit was with lepers at a settlement on the Opi River. Both she and Prince Philip shook hands with the sufferers, doing 'more to conquer man's fear and hate of the disease than any other single act', according to one official.

The daft trumpets in this picture are terrific. You can almost hear the sort of nasal noise they make. On 17th February 1956 the Queen and the Duke of Edinburgh arrived at the Emir's Palace in Kano, the northern Nigerian camel caravan terminus on the southern edge of the Sahara. Kano, a Mohammedan city, is the traditional capital of northern Nigeria. The Queen and Prince Philip were met there by the Emir who was resplendent in green and gold. He had a mounted escort who wore armour designed in the days of the Crusades. A number of terrific anecdotes came out of this trip. My favourite is the story of the Governor General's wife who slept in the royal bedroom at Government House in Lagos the night before the Queen, to test the brand new air-conditioning brought in for the royal visit. Unfortunately the local operators of this system were a trifle over-enthusiastic and she woke up shaking violently to discover that the temperature had dropped to just below freezing.

Opposite: The Queen, the Duke of Edinburgh, Prince Charles and Princess Anne pose on board *Britannia* in 1956. They had a rough crossing over the North Sea on their way to Sweden in the Royal Yacht so stabilisers were fitted. Once in Stockholm the yacht's role as a mobile palace came into being. One anecdote from that trip sticks in my mind. The Swedish chef asked a member of her household what the Queen liked for breakfast. 'Eggs' was the answer, so eggs it was. For her first breakfast in Sweden the Queen was faced with omelettes, poached eggs, eggs scrambled, fried and boiled too, in an effort to tempt the royal palate.

Opposite: Following a busy day of engagements on the second day of their state visit to Denmark on 22nd May 1957, the Queen, the Duke of Edinburgh, King Frederik IX of Denmark and Queen Ingrid of Denmark went to a gala performance of ballet at the Royal Theatre Copenhagen. The links between the Danish royal house and the British have long been strong. The Duke of Edinburgh, although a Greek prince, is actually of Danish stock, being a Schleswig-Holstein-Sonderburg-Glücksburg, the Danish royal line, once called the greatest exporting royal family this century. My own links come from my mother's marriage to Prince Georg of Denmark, a cousin of King Frederik. When I photographed King Frederik in 1964 I discovered that he was a connoisseur of tattoos. We had both been to the same artist, Mr Birchett in Waterloo Road, though I only sport one rather quiet tattoo while he is covered with them.

I love this marvellous picture of the Queen leading in her filly Carrozza after winning the Oaks on 7th June 1957. It has such a lot; from the wonderful composition, with the rein linking the Queen to the filly ridden by twenty-one year old Lester Piggott, to the slightly off-balance Noel Murless and those two hard-faced stable lads in the middle. These were some of the headiest of the Queen's days on the turf. Just three years before she had topped the owners' table with winnings of over £62,000 from thirty races. She is famous for her enthusiasm. A favourite quote is: 'If it were not for my Archbishop of Canterbury I should be off in my 'plane to Longchamps every Sunday.' Though Prince Charles talking in 1979 was not quite so kind: 'Whenever I back one of my mother's horses it is always a total disaster. I keep well out of that and advise you to do the same thing.'

Opposite: Although not a photograph this is one of the most compelling images of the Queen in the first decade of her reign. It is an oil painting by Grace Wheatley, called *The Crown*, painted in 1959. This allegory was commissioned by the theatre impressario Emile Littler to go with *The Prince*, a picture of the Duke of Edinburgh, and *The Statesman*, one of Sir Winston Churchill. On her first Commonwealth tour after her coronation the Queen set out some of her intentions for her reign: 'Some people have expressed the hope that my reign will mark a new Elizabethan age. Frankly, I do not myself feel at all like my great Tudor forbear, who was blessed with neither husband nor children, who ruled as a despot and was never able to leave these shores. But there is at least one significant resemblance between her age and mine. For her kingdom, though small it may have been by comparison with her European neighbours, was yet great in spirit and well endowed with men who were ready to encompass the earth.'

The Queen, the Duke of Edinburgh, Prince Charles, Princess Anne and seven month-old Prince Andrew sit in front of Balmoral Castle in September 1960. Prince Andrew, named after his paternal grandfather Prince Andrew of Greece, had been born at Buckingham Palace on 19th February 1960. He has been to Balmoral every year since then, as the Queen without fail spends her summer holidays there. Balmoral is really the creation of Prince Albert and Queen Victoria. Much of their own interior decoration survives. Most of the present generation of the royal family has learnt to stalk and to fish on the estate.

Above: The Duke of Edinburgh, Princess Anne, President Dwight D Eisenhower, the Queen, Prince Charles and Ike's son Captain John Eisenhower pose at Balmoral in September 1959.

Left: Richard Nixon, Eisenhower's Vice President, escorts the Queen during her visit to the United States two years earlier.

Opposite: This is quite lovely. The quality infers that it was probably shot with a 5″×4″ plate camera, almost certainly a Speed Graphic. The absence of wind-ons, let alone motor drives, meant you had to get it right, like wedding pictures. They'd shout 'Here love! Look over here!' and the Phoom! as the flash exploded. At the end of May 1961 the Queen and Prince Philip went on a two day visit to the north-west of England, carrying out a number of engagements in Manchester and Liverpool. Here they wave happily as they leave Liverpool after attending *Snow White and the Seven Dwarfs on Ice*.

Opposite: The Queen on a bejewelled howdah in Jaipur in India on her tour of 1961. On her arrival in the country, her first visit since independence fourteen years before, she said: 'I am thrilled to be here. To all India I bring a greeting of goodwill and affection from the people of Britain.' Of course Lord Curzon's words of the beginning of the century – 'As long as we rule India we are the greatest power in the world.' – were still echoing around Britain. But as the Queen's father said in his 1948 Christmas broadcast: 'Our Commonwealth has been subject to the laws of evolution. But it is stronger, not weaker, as it fulfils its ancient mission of widening the bounds of freedom wherever our people live; and, for myself, I am proud to fulfil my appointed share in that mission.'

Here the Queen and the Duke of Edinburgh pose in front of the Taj Mahal at Agra. The Mayor of Delhi offered the royal couple the compliment 'May you live 1,000 years and may each year consist of 50,000 days,' in his welcome speech. Extraordinarily the Queen's first visit to the country coincided with the Republic Day celebrations, a day which the Mayor of Delhi reminded her reflected the 'long history of conflict' between the two countries. But he added, 'that conflict was ended in a unique manner honourable to both our country and yours. The evidence of the welcome we give you is far greater than the words used in this address. The evidence is spread out all around us'. 400,000 people listened to that speech.

For part of their trip to India the Queen and the Duke of Edinburgh were the guests of the Maharaja of Jaipur who stands on the Queen's right. The Maharanee is on her left. Prince Jaga-Singh has his foot on the animal's head. The Queen is here seen holding her 16mm magazine-loading ciné camera after the shoot in Jaipur when Prince Philip stopped a tiger. It was 9′ 8″ long and after the skin was cured at Bangalore it was sent to Windsor. Of course the subject would be totally unacceptable today. Even thirty years ago it angered some when it was printed in the newspapers. The Duke of Edinburgh had to excuse himself from another shoot he had been asked on by saying he had a whitlow on his trigger finger.

Opposite: A historic moment as the Queen, the Duke of Edinburgh and Pope John XXIII pose in the Vatican on 5th May 1961. The Pope is wearing the most exciting slippers. The Queen donned for the occasion a long-sleeved dress of black lace over black satin, with a headdress and veil of lace and tulle. She gave him an ebony walking stick, and his present in return was twenty gold coins which had been uncovered in the Catacombs. This picture marked the end of the Queen's three day state visit to Rome where the Italians, knowing her love of racing, won her heart by changing the date of their Derby so that she could be there to watch it.

The official state portrait of the Queen above was painted by Pietro Annigoni in 1956. It was commissioned by the Worshipful Company of Fishmongers and now hangs in Fishmongers Hall. It expresses the optimism of the new Elizabethan age. The photograph opposite, taken by Beaton in the 1960's, links the two decades rather well. Annigoni, born in 1910, owed his introduction to the royal family to the

Duke of Edinburgh's cousin Queen Helen of Roumania. In this picture Beaton has used peculiarly hard lighting. He said of it himself: 'There have been so many pictures of the Queen in tiaras, orders and crinoline that I felt I must try something different. I asked Martin (Sir Martin Charteris, the Queen's private secretary) if a deer stalker cloak would be suitable. No he didn't think so but what about an admiral's cloak? navy blue serge.'

1962–1972

'THE DEMOCRATIC STATE'

> *'The role of the constitutional monarchy is to personify the democratic state, to sanction legitimate authority, to assure the legality of means and to guarantee the execution of popular will. My ardent desire is that no-one among my peoples is subject to coercion.'*
>
> The Queen, to the Provincial Legislature in Quebec 1964.

The Queen is pictured opposite on 26th June 1968 at the Royal Commonwealth Society's Centenary Garden Party at Marlborough House. In a magazine article some years earlier Baron Altrincham of Tormarton had called the royal family 'tweedy'. My cousin, Lord Strathmore, even threatened to 'shoot the bounder'. However the controversy contributed to a sea change which washed over the royal family throughout the 1960s. Their image was changing and the last of the Victorian attitudes ebbed away. Princess Alexandra summed it up towards the end of the decade: 'Nowadays we have to compete with Elizabeth Taylor and the Beatles.'

The Queen led the change. She had been the one who wanted cameras in Westminster Abbey for the coronation despite her advisers' objections. Now she wanted lenses to come further into her private life. The culmination of this policy was Richard Cawston's *cinéma-verité* film for the BBC, first shown in 1969, which changed what the world thought of the monarchy for ever. It showed the professionalism of the royal family, and generated sympathy for their huge workload. Royal portraiture was never to be the same.

But there were other more subtle changes at Buckingham Palace. Every year since Christmas 1957 the Queen's speech has been televised; the presentation of debutantes at court ended after 1958; and the Queen and Prince Philip instituted their practice of holding informal lunches with ordinary people once a week. She also ended the practice of her children having to bow and curtsey to her.

What took longest to adapt was the relationship between the press and the Palace. Commander Richard Colville, the press secretary from 1947 to 1968 was 'not,' as he told a Canadian journalist, 'what you North Americans call a public relations officer'. He managed to protect his royal charges as effectively as any household regiment, but he left an air of wariness when he departed. This has settled down now into a well-practised cycle of Palace and press treating each other politely, press overstepping the mark, and then a slow haul back to being polite again; and that way everyone knows the form. In the 1960s only the first tentative steps were being taken in this direction.

Above all the Queen wanted her children kept out of the limelight. She was prepared to open doors, but not to admit a flood. While they were at school that was relatively simple, but in 1967 Prince Charles went up to Cambridge and became public property. The Queen and Duke broke barriers with their children's education by sending them away to school. Gordonstoun in Prince Charles's day had a spartan atmosphere. When Prince Philip was asked how his son was getting on he answered, 'Well, he hasn't run away yet.' But situated in the wild country to the south of Moray Firth it was firmly out of the eyes of the world's press.

This move reflected the process of relaxation which Britain underwent in the sixties. It was not a decade, though, into which the royal family fitted quite comfortably. With only a few exceptions they did not find the moving and shaking, the mini-skirts and jeans, at all natural. Prince Charles trod an uneasy path through his course at Cambridge; and so, to a lesser extent did his younger brother Edward in the 1980s.

Prince Charles was fifteen, Princess Anne thirteen and Prince Andrew four when Prince Edward was born in March 1964. This was the *annus mirabilis* of royal births. Three days before Prince Edward appeared Princess Alexandra gave birth to her first child, James. Lady Helen Windsor was born to the Duchess of Kent on 28th April, and, on 1st May, Princess Margaret bore her second child, Lady Sarah Armstrong-Jones. This was a record four royal births within four months. The quartet were to have a combined confirmation party at Buckingham Palace fourteen years later, and in 1985 the Queen threw a sumptuous 21st birthday party for them at Windsor Castle.

A few months after Prince Edward's birth the Queen and Duke went to Quebec despite threats from French-Canadian separatists. Later on that year they travelled to war-torn Sudan. Luckily the government and rebels managed to call a truce for the duration of their stay. The royal couple stopped at nearby Ethiopia to see Haile Selassie. It is quite remarkable how few royal visits are called off. Once the Queen has decided to go somewhere she usually insists on going whatever disruptions may be taking place.

Early in 1965 a great wound was healed. The Queen visited West Germany to become the first British monarch to set foot there since before the Great War. One headline thundered 'Your Majesty, Germany belongs to you'. Another hatchet was buried when Emperor Hirohito of Japan came in state to London in 1971 causing a great storm of controversy. Lord Mountbatten suddenly discovered a prior engagement which prevented him from being at the state banquet.

Winston Churchill's funeral took place in 1965. It was remarkable for being the state funeral of a commoner and was attended by the Queen. I remember him coming regularly to School Songs at Harrow, an annual concert, given by the school for Old Harrovians. I was one of the young men bawling out the verses lustily. But one sticks especially in my mind for the tears which rolled down the great man's cheeks. 'Five hundred faces and all so strange! Life in front of me – home behind, I felt like a waif before the wind, Tossed on an ocean of shock and change'.

The Princess Royal died this year too. Mary, the Princess Royal, the only daughter of King George V and Queen Mary, was born in 1897. In 1922 she married the 6th Earl of Harewood. She always took life seriously. Her favourite brother, the Prince of Wales, said of her in 1919: 'I don't feel that she is happy. If only she would confide in me I might be able to do something. But she never complains. The trouble is that she is far too unselfish and conscientious. That's why she was so overworked at her lessons. When my brothers and I wanted her to play tennis she used to refuse because she had her French translation to do, or she hadn't read *The Times* that day. Is that normal for a girl?'

1965 ended with the Queen presiding over her first Christmas at Windsor since her coronation. Until then Christmas had been customarily spent at Sandringham. Since then she has alternated between Sandringham and Windsor. The shooting in Norfolk is the attraction. But the family was growing and Windsor has more rooms. Between 1975 and 1977 Sandringham was heavily refurbished when ninety-one of its room were pulled down to leave a mere 270. Windsor Castle is now undergoing extensive redecoration and structural work until the end of the century.

The Queen launched her namesake, the Cunard liner *QE2* in September 1967. She was built at John Brown's Yard on the Clyde. Her name had been kept secret until the moment it fell from the royal lips. It was meant to be called *The Queen Elizabeth*, but acting on a last minute impulse, the Queen said the words '*Queen Elizabeth Two*'. She carefully avoided the words '*Queen Elizabeth the Second*'. She was not naming the great ship after herself for that might have offended the Scottish shipwrights who had built her. Some Scots do not acknowledge the succession of the Tudor Queen Elizabeth I. So the Queen was merely saying that this was the second Cunard ship bearing her name.

Princess Marina died in 1968. With her husband, Prince George, Duke of Kent, she had been a leader of style in the 1930s, though in fact she was essentially a shy person, and preferred spending time with her children rather than in society. The Duke collected silver, paintings and furniture, in their two homes, Coppins, in Buckinghamshire, and 3 Belgrave Square. He had had a troubled upbringing and she a relatively poor one coming from the Greek royal family. Then, just as Princess Marina was sitting down to lunch, on Tuesday 25th August 1942, her husband was killed in a flying boat accident, en route from Scotland to Iceland. It plunged her into abject grief. With the country's austerity during and after the war, it was not considered right to grant the bereaved Duchess any monies from the Civil List, however popular and hard-working she was. Her husband's fabulous collections were sold off to raise some capital. The Queen however allocated a proportion of the Civil List to the Kents as soon as she could; although Prince and Princess Michael continue to receive no part of it.

For her last important public act of the 1960s the Queen invested her son Prince Charles as Prince of Wales at Caernarvon Castle. Lord Snowdon ably stage-managed the event which took place on 1st July 1969. He had become Constable of Caernarvon in 1963 and for this occasion worked with Carl Toms, the stage designer, and John Pound of the Department of the Environment. Their desire was to keep the 13th century castle as serene and uncluttered a backdrop as possible. This no frills approach is the hallmark of Snowdon photography too.

Later on that year Prince Charles celebrated his 21st birthday. Some 400 guests came to Buckingham Palace for the party. It started with Yehudi

Menuhin and the Bath Festival Orchestra playing Mozart and Haydn, and then there were fireworks in the garden. A large number of ambassadors left after this, but 150 of the Prince's younger friends and relations bopped to a band until 3 a.m.

The Queen committed herself to bringing the Prince of Wales forward as a member of the firm. He took his finals in 1970 but by then had already been introduced to the House of Lords, where in scarlet robe, ermine and gold he had pledged allegiance to his mother the Queen and 'her heirs and successors'. He also became a member of the Privy Council. He accompanied his parents and sister on a tour of New Zealand and Australia in his Easter vacation of 1970.

One of the notable moments for the Queen on this trip was her 44th birthday on Snapper Island, part of the Great Barrier Reef. It was later related by John Gorton, then Australian Prime Minister: 'Half the crew went ashore before us to spray everything so that there were no mosquitoes or sandflies, The chef started grilling spits and handing food around – a real de luxe picnic. It started quietly but soon developed into a lot of fun. Somebody decided everybody should be thrown into the water. Princess Anne was thrown in. Then Prince Philip. I was sitting next to Her Majesty. I was about to throw her in but there was something about the way she looked back. . .'

The Queen's visit to Canada in 1971 was linked to the centennial celebrations of British Columbia. She had a stinking cold, but managed to fulfil up to eighteen hours of public engagements a day for ten days. There was a moment of mirth for her and Prince Philip when at a rodeo at Williams Lake four stampeding bulls chased members of the press over a fence. Later that year she went on a hugely successful tour of Turkey. In Izmir the natives threw hundreds of flowers at her car on her drive from the airport.

The year 1972, which saw the Queen in South-East Asia, France and Yugoslavia, was one of those up-and-down years I have mentioned. Unfortunately a number of members of the royal family died. The Duke of Windsor died in Paris aged 77 in May. The Queen had taken the opportunity to visit her uncle during her state visit a month earlier. Sir Alexander Ramsay died in October. But the most tragic was the death of Prince William of Gloucester in a flying accident near Wolverhampton when he was only 30. His father, the old Duke of Gloucester, was to die two years later aged 74.

For me 1972 was a rewarding but highly nervewracking year. I came on the Queen's tour of the East on board *Britannia* and then later on I was invited shooting, with both gun and camera at Balmoral. The pictures which came out of these two trips have been some of my great successes.

The Queen has her pockets checked by an equine pal. She developed her absorbing love of horses one autumn at Balmoral while still a girl. Up until then her ponies had been groomed and tacked up at her pleasure. She learnt pony welfare and management, helped by the animal she had, called Jock. A picture of that pony taken some years later at Windsor has on the back in her hand-writing: 'Jock – who taught me more than any other horse.'

This picture by Karsh in 1967 is technically brilliant, but he has managed to capture both a light and an assistant in the mirror in the background. One of the problems with Buckingham Palace is the amount of wall space occupied by enormous mirrors. Not only do one's assistants have to move around like snakes but it affects the quality of the light which is frequently being reflected from several directions at once. I too have suffered from the royal mirrors.

Opposite: Women are not looking for 'character' in their photographs. They want to be flattered and elevated. Karsh took this in 1967 in the White Drawing Room at Buckingham Palace. He was ponderously trying to draw character out. Karsh's technique is to prepare himself for a session with anecdotes about his sitter. He asks his subject a provocative question just before he releases the shutter. King George VI once told the photographer Baron that a sitting for Karsh was a tremendous ordeal.

The Queen, riding the police horse Doctor, is at the head of the Brigade of Guards, returning to the Palace after her Birthday Parade, the Trooping the Colour, in 1963. I had recently left the army, so this picture is highly evocative for me. I had marched up there myself only two years before. Doctor, a quiet little grey, was second choice of mount to the chestnut Imperial, which had some foot trouble, and eventually had to be put down. When King George VI revived the Birthday Parade after the war he decided that his daughter, the heir presumptive, should ride half a length behind him. She was trained to ride side-saddle for it by the late Mrs Archer-Houblon.

Mick Jagger used to call Beaton 'Rip Van Withit'. In this portrait of 1968 Beaton is at his trendiest. He said of the day he took it: 'The Queen was in a good mood – or still had the remnants of a good mood on her, for she gave off, to the crew – unaccustomed hoots of laughter followed by a giggle. She also has developed a manner of making quite a lot of faces – grimacing and showing vitality.'

Opposite: Karsh's portrait of 1967 is not a feminine picture. He is happier photographing men. He first set up as an independent photograph in Ottawa. He had a great stroke of luck with a commission to photograph the Prime Minister of Canada, Mackenzie King, whose rather bland face he managed to make look almost regal. King showed his gratitude by introducing a steady stream of statesmen to Karsh's studio, and it was there that his famous 'bulldog' portrait of Churchill was taken and his success assured.

Opposite: The Queen reads her speech from the throne to the House of Lords at the Opening of Parliament on 3rd November 1964. Just two and a half weeks before, Labour, under Harold Wilson, had won the election. Wilson had had to go to the Palace to kiss hands, and for that he declined the morning dress and turned up instead in a suit. The Queen, he reported later, amazed him by her professionalism. She ignored the kissing of hands procedure and got straight down to business. What was Wilson's new Chancellor going to do about the £800 million balance of payments deficit? What of this new town planned for Buckinghamshire? – the one now known as Milton Keynes. In his retirement speech a dozen years later he told the House of Commons: 'I shall certainly advise my successor to do his homework before his audience and to read all his telegrams and Cabinet Committee papers in time, and not leave them to the weekend, or he will feel like an unprepared schoolboy.'

At the Opening of Parliament on 31st October 1967 in the Chamber of the House of Lords, the Lord High Chancellor presents the Queen's Speech to the Queen. On either side of her and the Duke of Edinburgh are Prince Charles and Princess Anne, attending the ceremony for the first time. Prince Charles had just gone up to Trinity College Cambridge.

The Queen's relationship with the media flowered in the
1960s, but to this day she is not quite at ease on
television. In the picture above she looks tense as she
records her Christmas Day Broadcast to the
Commonwealth. The pictures opposite are both stills
taken by Joan Williams for Richard Cawston's
documentary *The Royal Family* in 1969. In the lower one
the Queen is being filmed standing next to her trainer
Ian Balding. In the one above she is being filmed talking
to Tanzania's President Julius Nyerere, the longest
serving of the Commonwealth heads of government.

This is another of the great Beatons. It has something of a *Vogue* feel about it, something daring. It was taken to mark the Queen's 43rd birthday. Wearing a turquoise silk evening dress she stands against an English Regency sofa in the White Drawing Room at Buckingham Palace. The pearl and diamond tiara she is wearing was bought by Queen Mary in 1921 from the family of the Grand Duchess Vladimir of Russia.

Opposite: This picture is one of a series specially taken in the winter of early 1969 to show the informal life of Prince Charles, in preparation for his investiture later that year. Here he has a stroll with the Queen at Sandringham. The press office was putting particular emphasis on the less formal activities of the royal family, and was stressing the closeness of the family.

I was called upon to take my first official picture of the
Queen and the Duke of Edinburgh in 1966. It was to
mark the State Opening of Parliament, so I had to make
the scene suitably grand. I placed them and their
children on either side of the open doorway to give the
picture a sense of depth, and also so that I could slip in
some back-lighting. But I do not particularly like the
result. There is so much pomp and circumstance that
the subjects, apart from Prince Edward, are unrelaxed.
The best pictures that came out of the whole session are
from my reconaissance of the Palace. I was let loose to
look for a good spot, but I could not help noticing that I
was being shadowed through the corridors by a number
of burly men who watched my every move and muttered
darkly between themselves. As it turned out they were
not plain-clothes detectives, but electricians, sent to
make sure I did not fuse the building. I used them as
stand-ins for test shots, and they proved much better
subjects.

The Windsors join other members of the royal family to
unveil a plaque to Queen Mary at Marlborough House
on 7th June 1967. This was the Duchess of Windsor's
first ever official appearance at a public ceremony with
other members of the royal family. The Windsors had
come over on the *United States*, the flagship of the
United States Line owned by a cousin of the Duchess.
They had been met at Southampton by Lord
Mountbatten who had arranged for them to plant a tree
at Romsey in honour of their visit. The Mayor of
Romsey had to make a speech where he was told to
refer to the Duke as 'Your Royal Highness', and the
Duchess as 'Your Grace'. The Duchess repaid this snub
by not curtseying to Queen Elizabeth the Queen Mother
when they met. From left to right: the Duke of
Edinburgh, the Queen, the Duke of Gloucester, the
Duchess of Gloucester, the Duke of Windsor and the
Duchess of Windsor.

The Queen places on Prince Charles's hand the ring bearing the insignia of his principality as she invests him as 21st English Prince of Wales at Caernarvon Castle on 1st June 1969. Dotted around are a number of peers who carry various items of princely insignia, the then Home Secretary James Callaghan with his back to us, members of the royal family and the royal household and, behind them, members of the diplomatic corps. Lord Snowdon designed the event. His idea of the modern scenery contrasting with the old castle as a backdrop was clever, and suited the age well. The plexiglass canopy bore the emblem of Prince of Wales feathers in gilt and was supposed to be transparent for the benefit of television cameras.

Opposite: The Queen places the mantle around the shoulders of Prince Charles. The investiture was watched on television worldwide by some 500 million people with another 250,000 thronging the streets of the little Welsh town (population then 10,000). It was the biggest royal occasion since the coronation of the Queen in 1953 and the biggest royal event in Wales since the investiture of the last Prince of Wales, the Duke of Windsor in 1911. Prince Charles takes his job seriously. His hugely successful tour of the principality, including his efforts with the language with one term at University College Aberystwyth, was one of the main reasons the Welsh people did not opt for devolution in later years. One of Prince Charles's best comments about Wales concerns when he went to Llanelli. 'Can you say Llanelli?' asked the mayor. 'Of course', said the Prince, 'Llanelli'. The mayor wiped the royal saliva out of his eye and said 'Well done'.

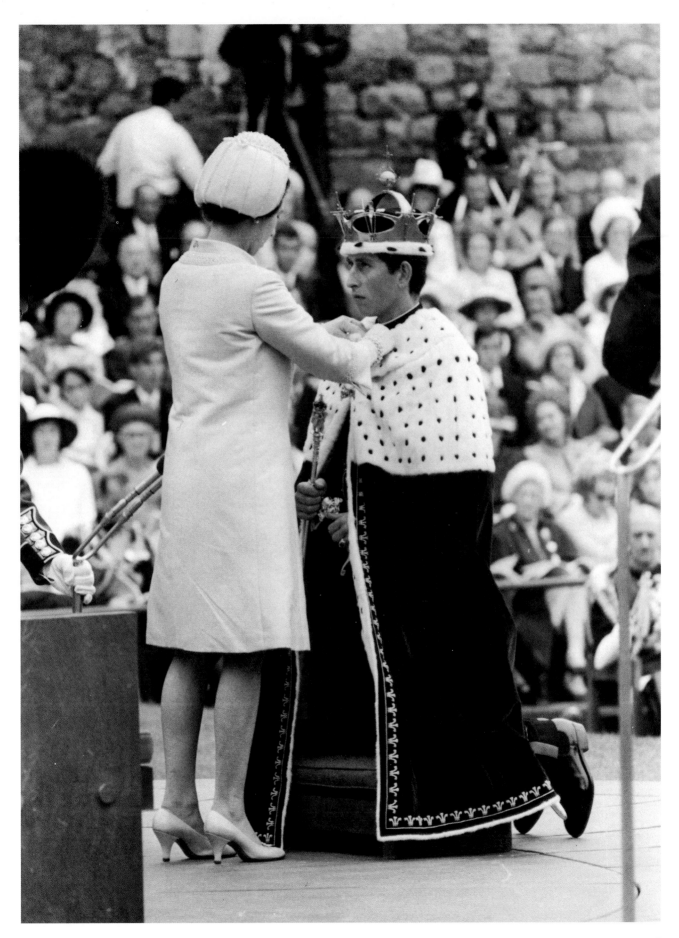

Opposite: This is my favourite picture of the Garter ceremony. With the billowing cloaks you can almost hear the organ voluntary pouring out of St George's Chapel after them. Just emerging into the sunshine is the late Lord Plunket, one of the Queen's greatest friends. He was orphaned when his father and mother died in an aeroplane crash. He was appointed Deputy Master of the Household in 1954 and served with consummate brilliance. He died, tragically, in 1975 aged fifty-one after a long illness. The Queen gave a site in Valley Gardens, Windsor Great Park, for a memorial to be erected to him.

This lovely picture of the Queen wearing the blue cloak of the Order of St Michael & St George shows how good the press can be at capturing an event. The order was founded by King George IV while Prince Regent in 1818. It honours British subjects working or serving abroad and is often awarded to diplomats. Recipients can put the letters CMG after their names. The great Foreign Office joke is: CMG 'Call Me God', KCMG 'Keep Calling Me God', and GCMG '*God* Calls Me God'.

This was part of a special series of pictures of the royal family taken during the summer at Balmoral in connection with the silver wedding anniversary of the Queen and the Duke of Edinburgh. Prince Philip has strong opinions on the subject of farming based on his work for conservation: 'It is not the ownership that matters, it is the sense of responsibility for the well-being of an estate in every way and so much enhanced by the feeling of continuity between generations of the same family. This kind of responsibility and emotional attachment cannot exist in the same way in professional management which is inevitably even more transient than ownership. Since I became involved we have had three Keepers of the Privy Purse, four Factors at Balmoral, two Agents at Sandringham and three Deputy Rangers at Windsor.'

Opposite: The Queen greets the King of Afghanistan, Muhammad Zahir Shah, on his arrival at Victoria Station on Tuesday 7th December 1971. Two years later the monarchy in Afghanistan was abolished and he was deposed. He had reigned for forty years, and his family for over 150 years. In the background are Field Marshal Earl Alexander of Tunis, Prime Minister Edward Heath, Foreign Secretary Sir Alec Douglas-Home and Home Secretary Reginald Maudling.

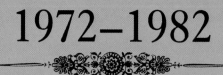

1972–1982

'COURAGE AND CALM DETERMINATION'

'We face grave problems in the life of our country, but our predecessors, and many alive today, have faced far greater difficulties, both in peace and war, and have overcome them by courage and calm determination. They never lost hope and they never lacked confidence in themselves or their children.'

The Queen's Christmas Message, 1981.

Opposite is one of a set of pictures I took at Balmoral for the Queen's silver wedding anniversary. The Queen is a highly respected breeder of labradors and keeps kennels at Sandringham. She also breeds cocker spaniels and, of course, the ubiquitous corgis. This kind of humanising picture may have set the great photographic interest in the royal family moving. But the forest fire of public demand for pictures began properly with the wedding of Princess Anne to Captain Mark Phillips in 1973.

It marked the beginning of a time when a larger group of photographers were invited to take the official portraits. Marcus Adams, Baron and Cecil Beaton had been the favoured few until then. But now a group including myself, Norman Parkinson and Peter Grugeon were asked in. The Queen wanted her family's image to appear more relaxed and informal, yet still retain that mystical mixture of dignity and exclusivity which keeps them royal. Beaton's theatrical backgrounds had had their day. A new generation of photographers established themselves, and for a variety of reasons. Norman Parkinson's favourite trick was to use his lamps to flatter, such as light angled from beneath the chin which takes years off a face. I worked hard to master the technique of backlighting. Snowdon correctly preferred simplicity. He liked to use natural light or, if necessary minimum lighting, relying on his wonderfully intuitive sense of what is the most appropriate pose and background for his subjects.

The industry of the less official photographer, the *papparrazzi*, took off too. Great murmurations flocked to the trees off the A93 along the banks of the river Dee at Balmoral in the summer. There they roosted in long mackintoshes, occasionally crashing to the ground in a clatter of camera equipment. They have always had short shrift from the Queen's family; and rightly so! Phrases like 'naff off' spring to mind. Even Richard Cawston from the BBC while making his royal family documentary was told 'Don't bring your bloody cameras so close to the Queen!' by the Duke of Edinburgh at naval decibellage.

But the *papparrazzi's* more respectable cousins, the staff photographers from the newspapers, have earned a certain grudging respect if nothing else for their tireless pursuit, something the royal family can understand, all hunting folk themselves. Prince Charles wished them a Happy Christmas one year, 'and a particularly nasty one to your editors,' he added. Having to stand out in the deep and crisp and even during the feast of Stephen for a fleeting glimpse of their quarry it was a sentiment many agreed with wholeheartedly, and I entirely endorse his comments.

The press find their feet most readily when there's a celebration to cover and in the ten years between 1972 and 1982 royal jamborees and bunfights were thick on the ground. The Queen's silver wedding in 1972 was followed speedily by Princess Anne's wedding, then there was the Silver Jubilee in 1977 and three years later the nation celebrated Queen Elizabeth the Queen Mother's 80th birthday. This, though, was nothing on the wedding of the Prince of Wales in 1981.

The Queen's silver wedding, stands out especially in my mind for the official pictures I had to take for it. This sort of work always inspires me with trepidation until I can detach myself by actually seeing my subjects through a lens. Sir William Heseltine, then the Queen's press secretary, told me in his inimitable Australian way over lunch at his club that a number of photographs were required for circulation throughout the year of the Silver Wedding anniversary. The tone of the pictures was to be unposed, almost photo-journalistic in tone, and they were to be taken during the first leg of the tour of the Far East in 1972. The prospect of sailing on the Royal Yacht was daunting enough; the idea of taking photographs whilst doing so seemed even more alarming, but it was, in fact, not just a privilege but a pleasure as well.

Sir Martin Charteris had the tour organized with the same eye-wincing polish as the yacht's brasswork. I crept around the outskirts trying not to interfere. Avoiding flash whenever possible, I tried to catch the Queen and her entourage in natural light and, after a few days, the click of my shutter became just another element in Britannia's smoothly running routine. Later in the year I was invited to Balmoral for the same purpose.

The service of thanksgiving for the anniversary took place in St Paul's Cathedral on 20th November 1972. The Queen said that evening: 'I think everyone will concede that today, of all occasions, I should begin my speech with "My husband and I".'

One year later Princess Anne's wedding to Captain Mark Phillips took place in Westminster Abbey. After months of speculation, including an official denial as late as March, the engagement had been officially announced at Balmoral on 29th May. A member of the household then commented, 'I know it sounds odd, but at that time they really had no thought of getting married.'

The 14th November, the birthday of both Prince Charles and the then Archbishop of Canterbury Dr Ramsay, was a sparkling autumnal day. Mark Phillips was supported by Captain Eric Grounds from his regiment, the 1st Queen's Dragoon Guards. Prince Edward and Lady Sarah Armstrong-Jones attended Princess Anne.

Television coverage of the wedding was unprecedented. Not only was the ceremony covered in full but cameramen were filming inside Buckingham Palace. Viewers were able to see many of the informal family moments such as the Queen telling Princess Anne to go out onto the balcony for the second time. 'Alright then,' and turning to Prince Edward, 'but get off my dress first.'

The three year gap between that wedding and the Silver Jubilee was notable for the growing interest in the royal family. There were more men in mackintoshes in the press tent at Badminton with film exposed of the royal family than of the horses, except when Princess Anne was riding. But although they lacked the practised finesse of today's ratpack there wasn't so much of the endless intrusion either.

This intrusion did not sit that happily with the security alert which flared up after the attempted kidnap of Princess Anne in 1974. Her parents, in Indonesia at the time, were shocked to hear that while returning from a charity film premier she was stopped in the Mall by a car swerving violently in front. The potential kidnapper was caught, but not until he'd plugged Chief Inspector Beaton, who recovered and was awarded the George Cross for gallantry. The man was later judged mentally deranged.

It did not affect Princess Anne unduly who for the next few years led the royal family in the eyes of the public. I spotted her potential early on when she took the record for a beginner riding a monkey-bike course around the park of my house Shugborough. She had won the *Daily Express* Sportswoman of the Year prize after winning the Raleigh Trophy for Individual European Three-day Event at Burghley in 1971. She took part in the European Championships in the Soviet Union in 1973, then West Germany in 1975. She won a place on the Olympic Team in 1976 but was thrown in the cross-country.

1977 was Silver Jubilee year. Although a few official functions had been planned to mark the event there was, to begin with, little public enthusiasm. Only one book was published to coincide with the anniversary and when the Queen and Prince Philip set off on their tour of the Commonwealth in the Pacific few people in Britain even knew of the anniversary. But the people of Western Samoa, Tonga, Fiji, New Zealand, Australia and Papua New Guinea certainly did. Their enthusiasm was infectious, and by the time the royal couple returned to Britain a groundswell of goodwill had gathered, culminating in the massive outpouring of loyal joy that occurred in the first week of June. Those of us who were around at the time remember the official events – the thanksgiving service at St Paul's Cathedral, the walkabout, the Guildhall lunch, the chain of bonfires across the country, the river pageant and fireworks display, the review of the fleet at Spithead – but even more, one remembers the informal events – the street parties, the town and village celebrations that involved every man woman and child in the country.

In the autumn the Queen and Prince Philip toured the Commonwealth again. This time it was to the Atlantic and Caribbean nations of Canada and the Bahamas. In her speech to the Commonwealth she said:

'It is easy enough to define what the Commonwealth is not. Indeed, this is quite a popular pastime. But from my own experience I know something of what it is. It is like an iceberg, except that it is not cold. The tip is represented by the occasional meetings of the heads of government and by the Commonwealth secretariat, but nine-tenths of the Commonwealth activity takes place continuously beneath the surface, and unseen. Cultural activities, professional, scientific, educational and economic bodies have between them created a network of contacts within the Commonwealth which are full of life and are much valued. And right at the base of the iceberg, the part which keeps the rest afloat, is friendship and communication, largely in the English language, between people who were originally brought together by the events of history and who now understand that they share a common humanity.'

To end the year perfectly Princess Anne gave birth to the Queen's first grandchild, Peter Phillips, in the Lindo Wing of St Mary's Hospital Paddington under the supervision of the Queen's gynaecologist Mr George Pinker. Peter was born on 15th November 1977. Other royal firsts associated with this birth included it taking place in a hospital, and he is the first child born so close to the throne (5th in line) without a title for 474 years, for his parents made a conscious decision at the time of their marriage to avoid those honours.

A notable year at the end of the decade was 1979. It was marked by the historic nature of the Queen's visit to the Gulf, but totally overshadowed by the death of Lord Mountbatten.

For the purpose of the Gulf tour she became an honorary man. The chauvinist Arabs realized that they could no longer ignore her. They needed Britain too badly. She was treated in Saudi Arabia as no other woman had or has since been – witness for example the treatment of the Princess of Wales ten years later, merely as the appendage of a powerful husband.

The assassination of Mountbatten was a tragedy beyond measure. He exerted enormous influence on the royal family, an *eminence grise*, and in some ways he was complemented by Queen Elizabeth the Queen Mother. She emphasized the Britishness of the Windsors and he their European roots.

The Queen Mother's birthday in 1980 was only a curtain-raiser for the events of 1981. The wedding of Prince Charles and Lady Diana Spencer, the first this century of an heir apparent, took place in St Paul's Cathedral too. Many reasons have been put forward why, not least because the building was designed by the husband of Diana's fourth cousin nine times removed. Diana was already unequivocally launched from the obscurity of the county set to super stardom, and 'the press,' as she observed, 'will hound me to my grave'.

It was a day of unsurpassed magnificence and ceremony. She fluffed his name at the altar itself, but whose heart did not go out to her at that time? There was a congregation of 3,500, but a worldwide audience of 750 million, a quarter of all the peoples on the earth.

I spent that day locked in Buckingham Palace, sweating out the last checks to my equipment for the group photograph, and reflecting that unless I got it right it could be the stickiest end to a much-loved career. The atmosphere of hysteria from the crowd outside reached even into the cool interior of the Palace. Prince Charles puts it well: 'I remember several occasions that were similar, with large crowds: the Coronation, the Jubilee, the various major national occasions. All of them were special in their own way, but our wedding was quite extraordinary as far as we were concerned. It made us both, and we have discussed it several times, extraordinarily proud to be British.'

The Queen fell about with laughter at the ducking I had on board *Britannia*, as I crossed the Equator for the first time by sea. The late Lord Plunket, Deputy Master of the Household, warned me when we neared the line that this might happen so I grabbed a camera as I was hauled out and covered in shaving foam by the crew. They hurled me into the canvas swimming pool that is strung up for members of the royal family to bathe in during the hotter parts of a voyage. The Queen filmed me with the ciné camera strung around her neck. Everyone has suffered this ignominy, even the Queen, when she was Princess Elizabeth, on *HMS Vanguard* in 1947. The initiated receive a certificate saying they are subjects of Neptune. When George V was told that the Prince of Wales, later Edward VIII, had been inducted he warned

his son to 'remember your station'. When it happened to me I was lucky my camera was sufficiently waterproof. Coming up for the third time I managed to press the shutter release. It is not the world's best picture, but it is a happy snap. It is proof that you should have a camera about at all times. I am a great fan of the disposable cameras that are now available.

The escorting frigate *HMS Arethusa* slips by and the crew line up on deck to cheer their Queen. This sail past is a traditional part of a tour on *Britannia*. Both *Arethusa* and an accompanying supply vessel did it, and it was a stirring sight. Each time the crews gave three cheers. Here they raise their caps as they do it. Later I requested the opportunity to look round the frigate. However, we could not slow down, so I was winched between the two as the waves crashed and boiled beneath me. Watching *Britannia* sail by is just as magnificent. The Duke of Edinburgh has said of her: 'Almost every previous sovereign has been responsible for building a church, a castle, a palace or just a house. William the Conqueror built the Tower of London, Edward IV built St George's Chapel at Windsor and Edward VIII built Sandringham. The only comparable structure built in the present reign is *Britannia*. As such she is a splendid example of contemporary British design and technology and much admired wherever she is seen, particularly on official visits overseas.'

From state duties in the morning, such as the picture on the right, taken at the bottom of the gangplank as she set off in full formality, to smiling at the cheers and flag waving on a walkabout, through to dinner, the Queen manages to remain tireless. By the time I had followed her around all day to take these I was more than a little haggard. It was on this flag-waving exercise in the Seychelles that I discovered how difficult being a photo-journalist is. I was joined by the press photographers and it was impossible for us all not to trip over and barge into each other as we tried to stay five yards ahead of the royal party. But the Queen is impressive not just for her coolness. She concentrates the whole time. Her attention never flags. She arrived at Mahé in the Seychelles from the Maldives where she had visited a hospital in the capital, Mali. The operating theatre there had gleaming new anaesthetic equipment, but none of the staff knew how to operate it. The Queen sent *Britannia*'s medical officer, Surgeon Lieutenant-Commander Ronald Snow ashore to show them.

In both these pictures you can see the horse-hair fly switch belonging to Jomo Kenyatta. He was one of the remarkable characters of the twentieth century. Already an octogenarian in this picture, he ruled Kenya with an iron hand. The Queen did not want any ceremony for her brief stop in Kenya on this occasion, the country where she had learnt of her accession. She wanted only to spend two hours there. So a member of her household told Kenyatta, in the way the Palace does things, the Her Majesty would understand if it was a 'quiet welcome'. Kenyatta replied personally: 'The Queen may understand, but the Kenyan people will not, and neither will our African neighbours.' In the end they compromised. It was a four hour ceremony. The President, wearing a suit to honour his guest, was surrounded by colourful natives who entertained the royal party with drums and dancing. In these pictures the Queen is boarding a VC10 of the Royal Flight, and I am about to miss it if I don't hurry! I was particularly pleased with the picture of the Queen standing on the steps, enhanced with a flourish of the presidential horse-hair.

Perhaps the Queen was working out the text of her
speech for the Opening of the Mauritian Parliament the
next day, when I took this picture. I did not want to
spoil the scene by using a flash so was quite lucky it is
not blurred. One of the red boxes stamped with her
name, which have dogged her for forty years, is on her
knees. She is talking it over with Sir Martin Charteris,
now Lord Charteris of Amisfield. He is wearing Red
Sea Rig, dress trousers and a cummerbund, but short-
sleeved shirt open at the neck, the correct evening dress
aboard *Britannia* in the tropics. His sense of humour and
prowess at deck quoits was much loved on that trip. He
was made private secretary to Princess Elizabeth in
1950, and, after a spell as assistant private secretary
when she became Queen, retired as private secretary
once more in 1977. His early years followed the familiar
course for a member of the royal household, through
Eton and Sandhurst, and after the war he was head of
military intelligence in Palestine. He was elevated to the
peerage and installed as Provost of Eton in 1978. He
delights in telling that one of his eighteenth-century
ancestors, Colonel Francis Charteris, was cashiered from
the English army for cheating, dismissed from the Dutch
army for theft, convicted, though later pardoned, for
rape and was a noted gambler of his day.

This group photograph was taken at Balmoral where I had been invited to take a few more pictures to mark the Queen's silver wedding anniversary. We had just been out shooting, and I knew I had to take that picture then, even though the gloaming was drawing in, for it was my only chance to catch the family together. It is probably because it was done so informally that the result looks, I think, pleasantly relaxed and casual. It is helped by the all-pervading freshness of Scotland, a blowy quality which the Queen with her Scottish mother can appreciate more than most. When Queen Victoria first visited Balmoral in 1848 she wrote in her journal: 'All seemed to breathe freedom and peace, and to make one forget the world and its sad turmoils.'

Opposite: I wanted to take a portrait of the Queen in the grounds of Balmoral. They are large, so I asked her first where she thought a picture like this could be done. She suggested this waterfall on the burn called Garbh Allt. Any excursion into the grounds is accompanied by corgis. I set everything up and was blessed with the luck of one of them jumping onto her knee when she sat down. I took the shot at once. I was a little disappointed when the films were processed because initially the picture seemed too chocolate-boxy. But it has grown on me and become one of the most widely used of the pictures from my stay in Scotland. I think it is her bright and relaxed expression which makes it so popular.

This picture is back-lit by the early evening light which I think helps it considerably. I was also consciously trying to move away from the stiff Balmoral pictures of the 1960s, and the impromptu nature of this session was useful. Balmoral itself has evolved during the Queen's reign. The Duke of Edinburgh has overseen the extension of Queen Mary's garden and the replacement on the 24,000 acre estate of the Ayrshire dairy herd with pedigree Highland cattle. The Duke devised a water garden and new trees have been planted, though not quite as many as by Queen Victoria who planted the Ballochbuie Forest at a cost of £100,000. That land was once sold by the Farquharson clan to the MacGregors for a tartan plaid. Queen Victoria had a stone put up there inscribed with the words 'The bonniest plaid in Scotland'.

Opposite: The Queen holds two shindies during her stay at Balmoral each year. I took this at the Ghillies' Ball where she is dancing the Dashing White Sergeant with a dashing red sergeant! A highland regiment is always stationed at Balmoral during the summer months. The Queen adores the reels and flings and she always starts the proceedings with an eightsome made up of other members of the royal family. She then makes sure that everyone in the room dances, especially the people for whom the dance is held, the estate workers. It is extremely important to know how to reel before taking up an invitation to Balmoral. I remembered with gratitude the agonizing dancing lessons my sister and I suffered at Windsor Castle in our youth. A flamboyant lady called Madame Marguerite Vacani made it her mission to teach us the skills of the ballroom. How we protested at the time, but once learned, never forgotten.

I was pleased with this off the cuff shot. The Queen and the horse seem to be bowing to each other. It was the day I accompanied the Queen around the estate on horseback. I am, of course, not a cavalry man at all, and weighed down with cameras *and* trying to make conversation the whole thing looked like being an ordeal. Luckily I coped without crashing to the floor. This picture was taken in the stable yard. Most of the stables at Balmoral have been converted to garages, but there are still two blocks for the various ponies and larger beasts the royal family use. There is also an assortment of traps, game carts and dog carts, as well as the Balmoral dog cart which was presented to the Queen in 1966 and which the Duke of Edinburgh drives around four-in-hand.

Although it might seem as if the Queen is pointing at
Balmoral Castle, she was in fact showing me a cairn in
the distance. It was during our ride. The Queen knows
an extraordinary amount about the local history of the
place. As a truly family home there are many personal
stories attached to it. It was where she and the Duke of
Edinburgh became unofficially engaged in 1946. In
Queen Victoria's day the fourteen year old Princess
Victoria announced her betrothal there, to Prince
Frederick of Prussia, later Kaiser Frederick III, after he
gave her a sprig of white heather he had plucked during
their ride up Craig-na-Ban. Queen Victoria erected a
thirty-five foot cairn on the Craig 'To the beloved
memory of Albert the Great and Good Prince Consort,
raised by his heartbroken widow Victoria R'. Queen
Victoria used to enjoy riding in the local country.
Sometimes the royal family would set off and ride
incognito for many miles and sleep in inns. Once,
Queen Victoria recalled in her journal, they were nearly
spotted. She heard a Scottish woman observe: '"The
lady must be awful rich", as I had so many gold rings on
my fingers.' That was in the days before photography
became widespread and made famous people instantly
recognizable.

Even though I am credited with having photographed my own wedding in 1975, the picture was actually taken by Peter Kain (or 'Pedro', as he is usually known). I married Lady Leonora Grosvenor, eldest daughter of the late Duke of Westminster, in Chester Cathedral. This picture was taken at Eaton Hall, the Westminsters' Cheshire seat.

Back row, left to right: Earl Mountbatten of Burma, Lady Jane Grosvenor (now the Duchess of Roxburghe), the Earl Grosvenor (brother of the bride and now Duke of Westminster), the Duke of Westminster, me, the new Countess of Lichfield, the Hon Brian Alexander (my best man), Prince Georg of Denmark (my step-father), Sir Geoffrey and Lady Elizabeth Shakerley (my brother-in-law and sister), ex-King Constantine of Greece, and Prince Michael of Kent.

Centre row, left to right: Jonathan Shakerley, Princess (now Queen) Beatrix of Holland, Princess Margaret, the Duchess of Westminster, the Queen, the Earl of Burlington, Queen Elizabeth the Queen Mother, Princess Anne of Denmark (my mother), ex-Queen Anne-Marie of Greece, Princess Benedikte of Denmark and Nicholas Shakerley.

Front row, left to right: Lady Laura Campbell, Lady Tara Crichton, James Campbell, Selina Weld-Forester, Viscount Strabane, Amanda Lee and Lady Sarah Armstrong-Jones.

The wedding of Princess Anne to Captain Mark Phillips took place on 14th November 1973. Norman Parkinson was commissioned to take the official photographs. I studied his pictures, and those of his assistants, in preparation for my own version eight years later (see page 119) to work out the necessity of precise planning. It is vital to ensure that everyone in a wedding picture has their eyes open, are graded according to height as well as precedence, and are looking at the camera at the same moment. At the back are Princess Alexandra and Angus Ogilvy. Middle row, left to right: Crown Princess Beatrix of the Netherlands, ex-King Constantine of Greece, Prince Klaus of the Netherlands, behind Princess Alice Countess of Athlone, ex-Queen Anne-Marie of Greece, Sarah Phillips (obscured), Crown Prince Harald and Princess Sonja of Norway, Major and Mrs Peter Phillips, the Duchess of Kent, Captain Mark Phillips, Captain Eric Grounds (best man), Princess Anne, the Duke of Edinburgh, Princess and Prince Richard of Gloucester, the Queen, the Duchess of Gloucester, the Duke of Kent, Prince Charles, Queen Elizabeth the Queen Mother, Earl Mountbatten, Princess Margaret, Queen Sophie of Spain behind Prince Andrew, Lord Snowdon, King Juan Carlos of Spain, and Prince Michael of Kent. Front row, left to right: James Ogilvy, Prince Edward, Lady Sarah Armstrong-Jones, Marina Ogilvy, Viscount Linley, Lady Helen Windsor, and the Earl of St Andrews.

This picture of the Queen in the garden of Buckingham Palace is by Dmitri Kasterine, who was the first photographer to employ me fulltime. He now runs a successful studio in New York. He is one of the most vigorous people I know and photographic sessions with him can be a little exhausting. His speciality is black and white work, especially portraiture, but royal portraits today are always taken in colour. His past is bizarre. Not only does it include a spell as a wine merchant, an insurance broker, an airline pilot, and a racing driver, where his scarred face comes from, but he is also a prince, the son of a White Russian emigré. I had to hold a crown over his head at his Russian Orthodox wedding. I spent my apprenticeship with this man, poring over the work of acknowledged masters like Irving Penn and Richard Avedon, looking at models' eyes for the telltale reflections which tell you how a lighting effect has been achieved.

Opposite: The portrait of the Queen and the Duke of Edinburgh in the Grand Corridor at Windsor is undoubtedly Peter Grugeon's best shot. It was taken in 1975. It is widely used in embassies and airports, which is itself an important point. When I photographed the royal family of Bahrein every police station in the country had to have a copy. That's better than publishing a book! Prince Philip, who is in the uniform of an Admiral of the Fleet, won a prize as best cadet at Dartmouth and was mentioned in despatches during the war. He was granted indefinite leave in 1951 to undertake a tour with his wife. He never returned to the service, though the next year he was promoted to Commander, a worthy feat at the age of thirty-one. He had to pass all the necessary examinations. He failed one on Torpedo and ASDIC and the Admiralty was on the point of overlooking that, but he said plainly that 'if they try to fix it, I quit the Navy for good'. He was allowed to resit, and this time he passed.

94

The Queen signs the visitors' book on her visit to the
naval base Faslane in 1975. In the background hangs
one of the Karsh portraits. The Queen and Prince Philip
enjoyed the years when they were stationed in Malta
with the Navy and the Duke took command of *HMS
Magpie* in September 1950. He was a tough captain. He
made it clear that we wanted *Magpie* to be cock ship, the
best in the fleet, even though she was junior. He pushed
his crew of 186 to outstanding success in manoeuvres
and victory in six of the ten events in the annual regatta.
The fleet gave him the coveted plywood rooster which
he hoisted up his ship's short mast. Princess Elizabeth
was allowed to live on board the Commander-in-Chief's
despatch vessel *Surprise*. In a light moment she startled
enemy monitoring by signalling 'Isaiah 33:23'. The
Duke replied with '1 Samuel 15:14'. Message reads:
'Thy tacklings are loose.' Answer: 'What meaneth then
this bleating of sheep?'

With the Queen's Bodyguard of the Yeomen of the
Guard lining the route, the Queen and the Duke of
Edinburgh enter the Royal Gallery of the Palace of
Westminster to walk in procession to the Chamber of
the House of Lords for the State Opening of Parliament
on 24th November 1976. They are preceded by Field
Marshal the Lord Harding of Petherton who carries the
Sword of State and Lord Peart who bears the Cap of
Maintenance. Behind the pages of honour in the centre
is Princess Anne. The Queen and Prince Philip walk up
to the thrones and when seated she says to the
assembled 220 peers, 95 of their wives and the 50
ambassadors (which is the most the house can cope
with) 'My Lords, pray be seated'. The Lord Great
Chamberlain then raises his wand to the Gentleman
Usher of the Black Rod. He is the one who walks to the
House of Commons to summon the elected politicians to
hear the gracious speech.

The royal family, all together in Montreal for the 1976 Olympics. The Queen opened the games with the words, spoken in French and English, 'I declare open the Montreal Olympic Games of 1976 celebrating the twenty-first Olympiad of the modern era'. 70,000 spectators in the stadium sang the country's national anthem *O Canada*. Then the athletes marched in, led by Greece. Britain sent 370 sportsmen and women led by the yachtsman Rodney Pattison who already held two gold medals. Princess Anne was in the Olympic three-day event team. After a fall she came 24th which was disappointing, but as Prince Charles said, 'It's not everyday you can watch your sister with a chance of winning an Olympic gold'.

Opposite: This portrait by Peter Grugeon was taken in 1976 for the 1977 Silver Jubilee tour of the Pacific, and it marks the final chapter of his remarkable rise as a royal photographer, for he died shortly afterwards. In 1975 the need arose for an official portrait quickly. With great initiative the Palace rang Kenneth Warr, Secretary of the Royal Photographic Society, and asked for a recommendation. Kenneth thought about it and then said that they could do a lot worse than ask a local photographer from Berkshire, Peter Grugeon, whose professional work was concerned mostly with the weddings of Reading, but whom Warr had long admired. Grugeon was soon rather startled to be called to Windsor to take the photographs which made him famous. This one looks a little awkward, but Ken Warr's idea has otherwise stood the test of time.

The Queen and Duke of Edinburgh, having arrived on board the Royal Yacht *Britannia*, anchored at Suva in Fiji on 16th and 17th February 1977. They were on their first Silver Jubilee tour which took them to Western Samoa, Tonga, Fiji, New Zealand, Australia and Papua New Guinea. On the first day they met four chiefs in traditional costume which was followed by a swig of the local drink *yaqona* at Albert Park. The next day they went to other ceremonies at Labasa before rejoining the yacht.

Opposite: The Queen and Prince Philip were welcomed by King Taufa'Ahau Tupou IV and his wife in front of the palace on Tonga. He is the son of Queen Selote and a great character. I use the word 'great' advisedly. At twenty-six stone, when he came to the wedding of the Prince and Princess of Wales in 1981, he had to bring his own chair, as his mother had for the coronation in 1953. He enjoys his food and supposed there was no reason that the Queen should not too. At the banquet in honour of her visit that evening she was given a turkey, two lobsters, sweet potatoes, a pineapple, a watermelon and a coconut to go with a whole roast sucking pig *to herself.* Prior to Tonga the Queen had been to Western Samoa where she had been received by King Malietoa Tanumafili II. He had turned up in London unexpectedly the year before and had been rather surprised to learn that the Queen, on holiday in Balmoral, would be unable to see him. To soothe his hurt feelings she made him a Knight Grand Cross of the Order of St Michael and St George. In return he awarded her the Grand Order of Vailima, a brand new order named after his palace.

Opposite: The Queen and the Duke of Edinburgh on their way to the Silver Jubilee Service on 7th June 1977 at St Paul's Cathedral in the Gold State Coach. It was a memorable week as is shown by the noisy exuberance of these photographs. The excitement mounted throughout May. Men began to work on the decorations in Trafalgar Square. The Mall became a fluttering mass of great banners, and bonfires were built all over the country. *The Daily Telegraph*'s headline of 3rd June said all: 'Try Winchester Hotels, London Tourists Told.' At Windsor on 6th June the Queen lit the first of a chain of 102 bonfires that stretched across the country. And a flame was flown to Australia where further bonfires were lit. The next day a cavalcade set off from Buckingham Palace, pictured here, through crowds up to twenty people deep. It consisted of three successive carriage processions, preceded by the Household Cavalry. Outside Buckingham Palace there was a guard of honour made up of the Royal Navy, the RAF and my old regiment the Grenadier Guards. After the service at St. Paul's she went on a walkabout to the Guildhall where she lunched with the Lord Mayor and big-wigs of the City of London.

The Queen and Prince Philip returning to Buckingham Palace after their lunch in the Guildhall. They are in the 1902 State Landau, a carriage built for King Edward VII. The crowds for the return journey were, if anything, even more enthusiastic than those of the morning. The day ended as Big Ben struck midnight with the Queen and Prince Philip and members of the family appearing on the balcony at the Palace for one last time as crowds shouted 'More! More!' and 'We want the Queen!'.

The Queen chats to Lester Piggott after presenting him
with a prize for his victory on The Minstrel in the King
George VI and Queen Elizabeth Diamond Stakes at
Ascot on 23rd July 1977. The Minstrel was that year's
Derby winner too. The Queen's great hope for 1977
was her filly Dunfermline. Ridden by her new stable
jockey Willie Carson, Dunfermline had won the Pretty
Polly Stakes at Newmarket by four lengths, and then the
Oaks at Epsom. Again ridden by Carson she was up
against the favourite Durtal, owned by Robert Sangster
and ridden by Lester Piggott. Piggott came off and was
dragged by one stirrup for 100 yards, luckily unhurt.
Dunfermline was stopped twice but still went on to beat
Freeze the Secret by three-quarters of a length. Carson
said of it: 'To overcome all the interference we had in
the race and still win was in my view a marvellous
performance.' The Queen wasn't able to attend but
watched it on the television. Queen Elizabeth the Queen
Mother was there, though, and presented the prizes. She
rang her daughter to congratulate her on not only
owning but also breeding the Oaks winner. Later that
year the Queen was voted 'Racehorse Owner of the
Year'. Actually, this is quite an unusual picture. The
only other time I saw Lester (known as 'old stoneface')
smile was when my assistant Sara Heaton, who normally
keeps a rather reserved county façade, turned cartwheels
across the hallowed turf at Newmarket.

These pictures were taken on the 1977 silver jubilee tour of the Caribbean.

Above: The Queen and the Duke of Edinburgh wave as Concorde flies past the Royal Yacht *Britannia*. It was 1st November and the royal couple were nearing Barbados. They returned to England in Concorde the next day at the end of their tour.

Left: The Queen and Duke of Edinburgh were met by Princess Margaret and the Hon Colin Tennant and his wife Anne on the jetty at Mustique. Colin Tennant married Anne, formerly Lady Anne Coke, in 1956. He asked the photographer Anthony Armstrong-Jones to take the pictures and that was the occasion Tony met his future wife Princess Margaret. The first time I ever went to Mustique, before the airport was built, I landed on that rickety old jetty. Almost everything that has been built on that island landed there. It was demolished only recently. *Britannia* was well-known there, for Princess Margaret's house on the island was a favourite stopping point. I have a house there, though for a time stayed in a gatehouse I built on Princess Margaret's grounds.

The Queen talks to Herr Scheel at the splendid Schloss Brühl near Köln, on the first evening of her visit to West Germany in May 1978. There was some concern over her safety during this trip. There had been a number of serious political kidnappings in Europe, and West Germany had suffered badly from them. The security planned for the Queen's visit was intense. But Buckingham Palace staff who were alerted to the precautions reacted strongly. The following message was sent to German security advisers: 'Your proposal simply will not do. The Queen wishes to get as close to the ordinary people whenever she makes a walkabout and when driving wants to be seen by the citizens and not by a closed line of police. Please remember the Queen is a woman of civil courage who wants to greet people and

not be treated like a queen bee.' Her wish was granted. She was able to chat to the crowds through an interpreter, though the Duke of Edinburgh spoke fluent German.

The Queen and the Duke of Edinburgh stand with Queen Margrethe II of Denmark and her husband Prince Henrik on the balcony of the Brockdorff Palace in May 1979. The royal party arrived in Copenhagen earlier that week on board *Britannia*. This is interesting for being a picture of two queens and two consorts. All but Prince Henrik are descendants of Queen Victoria. He is a Frenchman, born Comte Henri de Laborde de Monpezat. He became a diplomat, and married Queen Margrethe in 1967. She succeeded her father, the tattooed Frederik IX, five years later. I spent part of my childhood in her company when my mother married her cousin. She is remarkably bright and holds degrees from five universities including Cambridge and the London School of Economics. She speaks four languages fluently and has a working knowledge of the martial arts. She trained too with the Danish Women's Royal Air Force. Her greatest passion is archaeology and she has been on digs in Rome, Egypt and Scandinavia.

Opposite above: Prince Charles, Lord Mountbatten and the Queen chew over a point at polo on Smiths Lawn within a few flying divots of Windsor Castle. Polo was one of Lord Mountbatten's great loves; he wrote the standard work, *Introduction to Polo*. His enthusiasm was inherited by his nephew the Duke of Edinburgh and by his 'honorary grandson' Prince Charles.

Opposite below: Cricket has never had sustained royal support though Prince Charles has been known to wallop leather with willow for charity, and the Queen makes an annual visit to the Lord's test. On 15th June 1978 the Queen shook hands with the 21-year old David Gower when she and the Duke of Edinburgh met the England and Pakistani cricketers. Introducing the English players was their captain Mike Brearley, second from left. Other players in the line are, from left, Clive Radley, Ian Botham, Chris Old and Phil Edmonds.

Lord Porchester, now Lord Caernarvon, and the Queen egg on their fancy for the 1978 Derby. Unfortunately her colt English Harbour came a long way behind the winner Shirley Heights. This, by Mike Maloney of the *Daily Mirror*, won best picture at that year's Martini Royal Photographic Competition. Photographers tried to copy this picture for years afterwards, but never quite as successfully. The Queen appointed Lord Porchester as her racing manager from 1st January 1970. His job was to represent her at race meetings, to advise and to take decisions when she was out of the country. He was a good choice having been involved in racing for most of his life, as well as being a personal friend of hers. He bred the famous colt Tamerlane. His seat, Highclere Castle, near Newbury, is usefully close to West Ilsley and Kingsclere where the Queen's horses are trained.

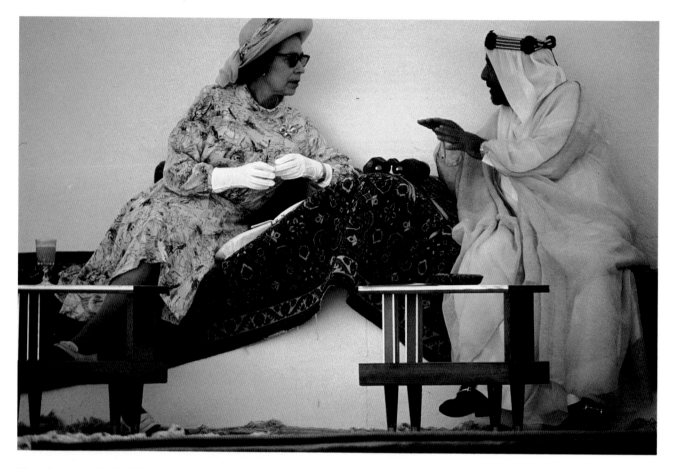

The Queen with the Emir of Bahrain at the races, during her six week tour of Araby early in 1979. I love his designer shoes! This was the tour where she made history by being treated as an honorary man in Saudi Arabia, a country which does not recognize women as anything more than chattels and where the women wear veils so thick it is impossible even to see their eyes. In Bahrain she was entertained by the Emir at his private race course. The cunning fellow allows only his own horses to compete, and the race card numbers are changed at the last minute to stop off-course betting. She also went to Kuwait, Oman, Qatar and UAE. In all these places she was presented with magnificent gifts of gold and jewels, gifts she is allowed to keep because what she gives in return has to be paid out of her own pocket. In this case she handed over silver salvers engraved with a picture of *Britannia* to each ruler, at a total cost to her of some £90,000. This picture won the coveted Martini Royal Photographer of the Year award for Tim Graham, who has become one of the best royal photographers around.

The Queen with the Duke of Edinburgh met her third
pope in October 1980. Here she listens to a speech
made by John Paul II in the throne room at the Vatican.
It was part of a tour of Italy and North Africa, including
the famous 'bloody' tour of Morocco, which was busy
even by her standards. She had two hours at Pompeii,
one at Carthage and only half an hour to drive through
Rome. In this picture the Queen is wearing a long dress
of black taffeta designed by Ian Thomas, a black veil, a
diamond tiara and the sash and star of the Order of the
Garter. It was appropriate that the Pope should give her
a facsimile edition of Dante's *Divine Comedy*, for it has
an illustration of the Garter worn by Edward IV during
the fifteenth century. In return she gave him a book
about Windsor Castle and a signed photograph in a
silver frame.

At Prince Andrew's passing out at Dartmouth Naval College the Queen inspects the parade and smiles as she passes her twenty year-old son on 1st April 1980. The gleam from his cap really is astonishing photographer's luck! Prince Andrew is a keen photographer and has even published a book of his pictures with the hope that it might encourage others to 'have a go' at the hobby. He recalls the time after the Falklands conflict that photography first struck him: 'The Argentinian soldiers looked dejected and faced a questionable future on being evacuated; the mess; the grime; the chaos; the number of people milling around in different uniforms, most of them with guns. It was a unique view. I wish I had a camera with me to record everything that was going on.'

Opposite: The Queen and the Duke of Edinburgh arrive at St George's Chapel, Windsor Castle, for the Garter Ceremony on 16th June 1980. It was a windy day, and promised rain later. It was the day Queen Margrethe II of Denmark was installed as a Lady of the Garter to join Queen Silvia of Sweden and Queen Juliana of the Netherlands. Two knights were installed to bring the numbers to twenty-five once more. Lord Mountbatten and Field Marshal Sir Gerald Templar had both died in the previous year. Their places were taken by the Lord Lieutenant of Devon, Field Marshal Sir Richard Hull, and Governor-General of New Zealand, Sir Keith Holyoake. Queen Elizabeth the Queen Mother also came, in her eightieth year, escorted by Grand Duke Jean of Luxembourg.

The Queen visiting the Royal Welch Fusiliers, of which she is Colonel-in-Chief, in Wiltshire in 1978. Her professionalism makes her one of the easiest people to talk to and her experience one of the most interesting. She said in her Christmas message later that year: 'It is far from easy to be cheerful and constructive when things around us suggest the opposite. But to give up the effort would mean, as it were, to switch off hope for a better tomorrow. Even if the problems seem overwhelming, there is always room for optimism. Every problem presents us with the opportunity both to find an answer for ourselves and to help others.'

The Queen poses with her new Prime Minister Margaret Thatcher at the stormy Commonwealth heads of government meeting in Zambia in 1979. The Prime Minister was involved in the public battle over the fourteen year-old Rhodesian problem, while the Queen worked quietly behind the scenes. Rhodesia was at last brought to legal independence. At the time this picture was taken the Queen was on a 15,200 mile trip, one of the most successful of her reign, during which she managed to cement the African factions of the Commonwealth, which had been boiling in post-independence bitterness. By the time she left one local newspaper compared her tour to the second coming of the Lord, another called her the Great White Mother of Africa. The *Zambian Daily Mail* eulogized: 'She has an extraordinary loving heart for every human being, regardless of colour. This vital quality, coupled with her warm heart, makes her a fitting mother of the world. In fact she could quite easily be elected Queen of the World.'

Just as it had for his parents, Prince Charles's romance
with Lady Diana Spencer began at Balmoral. On 24th
February 1981 their engagement was formally
announced and the wedding set for St Paul's Cathedral
on 29th June that year. If Prince Charles becomes King
his will be the first truly English Queen Consort since
Henry VIII's last wife, Anne of Cleves. Diana's father
had the necessary background in the royal household,
having been an equerry to King George VI and later to
the Queen. In this picture, taken to mark the
proclamation of her marriage, Lady Diana is already
revealing that delightful shy, conspiratorial smile that
has helped turn her into one of the world's super stars.

On the left the Queen chats to cub scouts during a visit
to Shetland in May 1981 and on the right to veterans at
a garden party at Holyroodhouse in Edinburgh two
months later. These terrific pictures are not well known
because during these months the attention of the press
was fixed firmly on the future Princess of Wales. The
very old or the very young usually feel at ease with the
Queen, whereas people in between are often too struck
to open their mouths. These two pictures say a lot for
the spontaneity of stills pictures as well. You could watch
these scenes a dozen times on video and not be
impressed. The Queen spends part of each year before
her holiday at Balmoral in official residence at the Palace
of Holyroodhouse, carrying out engagements in
Scotland. She holds garden parties, opens factories and
invests senior Scots with the Order of the Thistle. The
Order of the Thistle service takes place at St Giles's
Cathedral in Edinburgh, the chapel of the order. Helped
by his son, King James II and VII revived the order 300
years ago to be a Scottish equivalent to the Order of the
Garter. There are sixteen knights in addition to the
sovereign, unless any extra have been created by special
statute. King Olav of Norway was one of those extra
knights and the Queen made a state visit to Norway
from which she was returning aboard *Britannia*, when
she called at the Shetlands for the picture above.

On the right is an example of truly modern photography. It was taken with a long lens on a fast shutter speed to extremely high quality. The Queen is pictured at the Royal Windsor Horse Show on 15th May 1981. The show takes place on a large flat area on the banks of the Thames with the Castle a fabulous backdrop. Wearing headscarf and Husky jacket the Queen tramps from competition to competition like any country lady. She adores her horses and her dogs. Away from Buckingham Palace this is the life she seeks. Normally at Windsor and Sandringham she is up first thing in the morning and down to the stables where the groom already has a horse saddled up for her ride.

Having looked closely at previous wedding photographs I realized that to take this one I needed something special. Normally in wedding groups heads are obscured and people blink and look the wrong way. The answer was the Acme Thunderer which hangs proudly in a glass case in my office to this day. Just as everyone had assembled, having looked to see where they were to go on one of the charts I had scattered around the room, they were chatting noisily when I blew a referee's blast on that whistle, fifty-seven heads turned and, as you see, most found it quite funny. I took several more afterwards, which are a touch more formal, but this one is fun and has not been published so often.

Back row left to right: Prince Henrik and Queen Margrethe of Denmark, King Olav of Norway, James and Marina Ogilvy, Captain Mark Phillips, Angus Ogilvy, Princess Alexandra, Prince Andrew, Viscount Linley, the Duchess of Gloucester, the Duke of Edinburgh, the Duke of Gloucester, Prince Edward, Princess Alice, the Princess of Wales, the Duke of Kent, Ruth Lady Fermoy, the Prince of Wales, the Earl of St Andrews, the Duchess of Kent, Lady Jane Fellowes, Viscount Althorp, Robert Fellowes, Prince and Princess Michael of Kent, Princess Grace and Prince Albert of Monaco, Prince Claus of the Netherlands, Princess Gina and Prince Franz Josef of Liechtenstein.

Middle row: King Carl Gustav and Queen Silvia of Sweden, King Baudouin and Queen Fabiola of Belgium, Princess Margaret, Princess Anne, Queen Elizabeth the Queen Mother, the Queen, India Hicks, Lady Sarah Armstrong-Jones, Mrs Shand-Kydd, Earl Spencer, Lady Sarah and Neil McCorquodale, Queen Beatrix of the Netherlands, Lady Helen Windsor, Grand Duke Jean and Grand Duchess Josephine Charlotte of Luxembourg.

Front row: Edward van Cutsem, the Earl of Ulster, Catherine Cameron, Clementine Hambro, Sarah Jane Gaselee, and Lord Nicholas Windsor.

I caught this of the bride and bridesmaids in
Buckingham Palace just after my carefully planned group
photographs had been taken and everyone had broken
up. The new Princess of Wales is comforting the
youngest of the bridesmaids, six year-old Clementine
Hambro who is Sir Winston Churchill's great
granddaughter and was one of her charges at the
Montessori school where she worked. The other
bridesmaids in the picture are, from left to right Lady
Sarah Armstrong-Jones, India Hicks, and Sarah Jane
Gaselee. Lady Sarah, Princess Margaret's daughter, was
bridesmaid at my own wedding. India Hicks is a
granddaughter of the late Lord Mountbatten, and Sarah
Jane Gaselee is a daughter of Nick Gaselee, Prince
Charles's horse trainer. The other bridesmaid was
Catherine Cameron, daughter of Donald Cameron of
Lochiel and Lady Cecil Cameron, daughter of the
Marquess of Lothian who has been a Lord-in-Waiting
to the Queen and more recently Lord Warden of the
Stannaries and the Keeper of the Privy Seal of the Duke
of Cornwall, one of Prince Charles's appointments.

1982–1992

'THE RIGHT MESSAGES TO SEND'

> *'We have the means of sending and receiving messages, we can travel to meetings in distant parts of the world, we can exchange experts; but we still have difficulty in finding the right messages to send, we can still ignore the messages we don't like to hear and we can still talk in riddles and listen without trying to comprehend.'*
> The Queen's Christmas Message, 1983.

For my final chapter opener I have chosen a picture of the Queen accepting daffodils from some of the 5,000 British and Commonwealth schoolchildren who assembled outside Buckingham Palace on her sixtieth birthday 21st April 1986. Earlier she had listened to them sing *The Queen's Birthday Song* which had been composed for the occasion. They were accompanied by the band of my old regiment, the Grenadier Guards.

What of the rest of the last ten years? Photography has reached unmitigated heights of technical brilliance, though some photographers still lack subtlety and there are dressing-downs for editors who print pictures of pregnant princesses in bikinis.

The Queen has now reached her sixty-fifth birthday without retiring. She soldiers on without lessening her commitments. A table of engagements for 1990 published by *The Times* credited her with 570, second only to the Princess Royal who undertook 768.

Prince Andrew was involved in two of the big events of the 1980's. He flew helicopters in the Falklands in 1982, and married Sarah Ferguson in 1986.

Prince Andrew went out with the task force as a helicopter pilot attached to *HMS Invincible*. He spoke about his experiences after the conflict was over. Part of his job was to act as a decoy for Exocet missiles. These weapons can only fly under a height of twenty-seven feet, so helicopters are used to tempt them away from ships, and then gain height as they draw near. 'But on the day that *Sheffield* was hit, one Exocet was seen to fly over the mast of a ship, that is, well over twenty-seven feet. For the first ten minutes we didn't really know which way to turn or what to do. I knew where I was, and I was fairly frightened.' It was an unnerving time for the Queen and she was there with Prince Philip and Princess Anne at Spithead to welcome him back. During the conflict the Queen had spoken publicly of how closely she identified with the mothers of other servicemen. Prince Andrew said he couldn't have been in a better squadron 'They're absolutely fantastic. They've worked very hard, and I can only say that the squadron is a great squadron, and I'm glad I've served with her.' Prince Andrew's work picking up survivors of the *Atlantic Conveyor,* and the missing crew of one of *HMS Hermes*'s helicopters was highly praised.

Four years later he married Sarah Ferguson, the second daughter of Major Ronald Ferguson, Prince Charles's polo manager. The wedding took place at Westminster Abbey on 23rd July 1986. The bride confidently predicted that no one had ever seen a dress like it and she was right. The Mall was filled with people waiting for Prince Andrew to kiss the bride, and as before, but perhaps a little more flamboyantly, their hope was rewarded.

During the last decade the Queen has acquired four more grandchildren. Prince William appeared on 21st June 1982. His christening took place in the Music Room at Buckingham Palace on his great grandmother Queen Elizabeth the Queen Mothers 82nd birthday. It was the then Archbishop of Canterbury, Dr Runcie's, first royal christening. The new heir presumptive was named William Arthur Philip Louis. William was chosen, stressed Prince Charles, because he and Princess Diana like the name. He is a boisterous chap, currently at Ludgrove prep school near Windsor. He once called up most of the local emergency services with a playful dab of a knob at Balmoral.

Prince Harry was born on 15th September 1984 in the Lindo Wing of St Mary's Hospital Paddington. He is a quieter child and has just joined Prince William's old school Wetherby having been at Miss Mynors', a Montessori school in Chepstow Villas.

The Duke and Duchess of York are delighted with their young. 'She's changed our lives,' said the Duchess after Princess Beatrice's birth. 'Really, she's absolutely unbelievable. I'm very, very fortunate that she's so well and healthy. She is so incredibly placid and calm. I don't know where she gets it from – probably her father.' Now Princess Eugenie has joined her, and the Queen can expect more grandchildren. When it was announced that Princess Beatrice was on the way the Duchess said, 'It would be fun to have quite a few, wouldn't it'. At a reception recently Princess of Wales mentioned: 'I'd like three more babies – but I haven't told my husband yet. You see, I grew up in a family of four, but I would like one extra. I think five children make the perfect family.'

The Queen's most important constitutional act of 1982 was as Queen of Canada to proclaim the revised Canadian constitution. There had been years of fruitless debate as to what it should contain from the British North America Act of 1867 and the Statute of Westminster of 1931. This was complicated by the actions of the French-Canadian separatist groups. The Queen made sure she was closely informed about the state of play, and was delighted to be able to in some way help bring order when she signed the proclamation in Ottowa.

After attending the Commonwealth Games in Brisbane in October 1982 she and the Duke toured the South Pacific. In Funafuti in Tuvalu she was borne out of the water in her boat by highly colourful natives. That is one of the most famous images of the decade.

The next year she went to the Caribbean for a tour which took her through the Panama Canal and up the Pacific coast of the USA. There she made her highly publicised visit to the Reagans in California. And due to winter storms it proved impossible to use the Royal Yacht to go on to Canada; so she flew.

But *Britannia* found the sailing from Britain to Sweden much easier later in the year. The Queen went to visit King Carl XVI Gustav of Sweden who shares Queen Victoria as a common ancestor with both her and the Duke of Edinburgh. King Carl Gustav has broken with tradition in Sweden somewhat by marrying a commoner, Silvia Sommerlath. He has set quite a precedent too by declaring that in future the succession will pass to the monarch's eldest child, regardless of its sex. So his heir is his daughter, Crown Princess Victoria, even though she has a younger brother, Prince Carl Edmund. In 1985 King Carl Gustav was installed as a Knight of the Garter.

In November 1983 the Queen went on a return trip to Kenya, Bangladesh and India. In Kenya she revisited Treetops where she had been when she heard the news of her accession.

1984 was the anniversary of the D-Day Landings, an occasion which saw a great gathering of the allies on those beaches forty years on. In the words of her Christmas Day message of 1984: 'That occasion in Normandy was a memorable one for all of us who were able to be there. It was partly a day of sadness, as we paid our respects to those who died for us, but it was also a day full of comradeship and hope. For me, perhaps the most lasting impression was one of thankfulness that the forty intervening years have been ones of comparative peace. The families of those who died in battle and the veterans who fought beside them in their youth, can take comfort from the fact that the great nations of the world have contrived, sometimes precariously maybe, to live together without major conflict. The grim lessons of two World Wars have not gone completely unheeded.'

In 1987, as one of the most notable visits of the decade, she went to China, the first British monarch to do so. She saw Tiananmen Square which two years later was to become such a bloodbath. At the time her going there inspired great hope in the West that a special relationship between the two great imperial powers of the past was being forged for the future.

Another superpower which teeters on the brink of a visit by a British monarch is the Soviet Union. Despite its uncertain political future Princess Anne went there in 1990, possibly paving the way for the Queen to take up President Gorbachev's invitation of 1989. However, the Queen's sense of history is strong. Her grandfather was on the throne when their cousins the Romanovs were butchered by the Bolsheviks, and the Russian Tsar and Tsarina were the Duke of Edinburgh's uncle and aunt, so the British royal family has double cause to be wary of the Russian bear.

During the 1980s the Queen began to cross the Atlantic almost every year in private on the holiday to Kentucky, where the bloodstock thrives on the bluegrass. In 1991 she made her third state visit to the United States. No country outside the Commonwealth has previously had more than two. It is the sign of the continuing close relationship between Britain and America.

Alongside the Queen on all her tours has been the Duke of Edinburgh. Without his no nonsense approach to life the Queen would have found it hard to keep on top of her work. They share a sense of humour, of the ridiculous and an enormous sense of fun which when together sparks enthusiasm for tasks in hand. His has been a difficult job as consort. But together with Queen Elizabeth the Queen Mother he has been one of the firm foundations on which this reign of forty years has been supported, the constant for a monarch whose work itself is always to be constant.

The Duke of Edinburgh's keen interest in science is shared by the Queen. At the age of sixty-five her sense of the future is still strong. In her Commonwealth Day Message of 1991 she stressed the importance of technology: 'The Commonwealth, with its many tried channels of communication and consultation, is uniquely placed not only to enable member countries to keep abreast of scientific advances, but also to help them benefit from their practical applications. I believe that the Commonwealth tradition of quiet cooperation and its advantage of common language can make a special contribution to the practical application of science wherever it is most needed for the sake of human welfare as well as for the long-term health of our planet.'

Opposite: Pope John Paul II met the Queen in the early summer of 1982. During his crowded visit to Britain he found time to spend half-an-hour at Buckingham Palace where he had a special message – 'God bless your son' – referring to Prince Andrew who was on active service against Argentina in the South Atlantic at that time. The following day, after an ecumenical service at Canterbury Cathedral, Prince Charles talked for a time with the Pope and the Archbishop of Canterbury, Dr Robert Runcie, in the Deanery library. Prince Charles's marriage service included prayers by both the Roman Catholic Archbishop of Westminster and the Moderator of the Church of Scotland, and the lesson was read by the Methodist Speaker of the House of Commons.

On 4th August 1982, his great grandmother's birthday, Prince William Arthur Philip Louis of Wales was christened in the Music Room at Buckingham Palace. This picture was taken in the White Drawing Room, where the furniture has obviously been rearranged for the photograph. It is not normal for the sofa to be placed with its back to the fire, but there are five large windows overlooking the garden, and the light from them would have thrown strong shadows if the sofa had been in its normal place. As it is the photographer, Kent Gavin, was able to stand with his back to the light and used a little bit of flash. I noticed also that the ornate mirror which is usually over the fireplace, was replaced by a picture, so as to avoid the dreaded reflections.

This state banquet, above, at Windsor Castle marked
President Reagan's visit to Britain on 8th June 1982.
Reagan had the honour of being the first President of
the United States to be the guest of the sovereign at a
royal residence when he and Mrs Reagan visited
Windsor in June 1982. They stayed in rooms in the
Lancaster Tower. They were accompanied by US
Secretary of State General Alexander Haig and Mrs
Haig, and a staff of fifteen, all of whom stayed at
Windsor Castle as well. The Duke of Edinburgh was at
Heathrow Airport to meet the American visitors and
accompany them on their helicopter flight to Windsor
where they were greeted by the Queen and the Prince of
Wales. That evening the President was entertained at a
banquet in St George's Hall attended by many members
of the royal family, where they ate *Filet d'Aiglefin St
Germain* and *Supreme de Volaille aux Mangues*.

Next day the Queen and the President went for their highly publicized ride in the Windsor Home Park, with the Duke of Edinburgh driving Mrs Reagan in a four-in-hand carriage. The President looked as if he would have been more comfortable on a Western-style saddle. But it was at his own request that he should be able to ride one of the Queen's horses that the jaunt was organized in the first place, and the royal horses are not trained in Western-style riding. The Crown Equerry, Sir John Miller, declined the offer of a horse from one of the leading Western-style riders in the country, thus indicating that the President was quite prepared to ride on an English saddle.

President Kaunda and his wife pause with the Queen, the Duke of Edinburgh and Queen Elizabeth the Queen Mother before going in to a banquet in honour of the Zambian President on 22nd March 1983. Kenneth Kaunda became President when Northern Rhodesia became Zambia in 1963. In 1973 he introduced a new constitution abolishing all other political parties except for his own. In 1979 he hosted the troubled Lusaka Commonwealth Heads of Government Conference. He said afterwards of the Queen's work on the subject of Rhodesia: 'It's her personality, her thoughts towards mankind, which makes her such a welcome contributor to what goes on at these summits. At the Lusaka meeting in 1979 she played a very vital role. The Queen is an outstanding diplomat; that's how she gets things done.' He went on: 'There were criticisms about the conference being held in Zambia, especially from the right-wing members of the British press. The Queen took a personal decision to come.'

Opposite: The Queen watches the Duke of Edinburgh competing in the carriage-driving competition at the Royal Windsor Horse Show on 14th May 1982. She is carrying a Leica with an old-fashioned light meter. She is often pictured with either a Leica or a Rolleiflex. Sir John Miller, in charge of the Royal Mews, persuaded the Duke of Edinburgh to take up driving four-in-hands from Buckingham Palace Mews. Although not as racy as polo, carriage-driving is by no means sedate. Prince Philip took to it at once. He asked his old friend Sir Mike Ansell to look into turning the sport into an international competitive event with a proper set of rules. Ansell came up with a competition based on the three-day rider's event. In his book on the subject Prince Philip writes: 'Things kept going at an alarming pace. After a bit of arm twisting the Windsor Horse Show put on an international driving competiton for four-in-hands in 1971 and in the autumn of the same year the Hungarians organised the first European Championships.'

Here the Queen is borne out of the water on the island of Tuvalu in a scene reminiscent of Grace Wheatley's painting on page 38. It was during their tour of the South Pacific in October 1982. The Queen and the Duke of Edinburgh disembarked from *Britannia* in the royal barge. About half way from ship to shore they were met by canoes full of Tuvaluvians – about forty to each one. Tall chairs had been lashed to the middle of two of these boats for both the Queen and Prince Philip, and they transferred to these precarious craft to be paddled ashore. Then, the islanders stopped in the shallows, leapt out, and carried them on their shoulders up and into the village.

Opposite: In this lovely picture of the Queen on the Solomon Islands, it is the Prime Minister holding the protective parasol. It was on the hilly, thickly forested Solomon Islands that the Duke of Edinburgh made one of the outspoken comments for which he is notorious. Visiting a hospital in Honiara, he was appalled to learn of the island's high birth rate. 'Five percent! You must be out of your minds,' he fumed when told that that would lead to a doubling of the population by the end of the century. 'You'll have a massive economic crisis in twenty years' time and then blame everybody else.'

130

Opposite: The Queen met Mother Teresa of Calcutta at the presidential palace in New Delhi on 25th October 1983, during her tour of India. The dramatic shadows come from the television lights which so often hinder stills photography. This astonishing nun who has devoted her life to caring for the destitute of Calcutta, had already won the Nobel Peace Prize, when the Queen arrived to give her the Order of Merit. 'This is not for me,' Mother Teresa said afterwards. 'This honour is for the poor.'

In November 1983 the Queen returned to Treetops, where she had learned of her accession thirty-one years earlier. The original Treetops hotel had burned down in 1954 and had since been replaced by the building on stilts in the background. The Sagana Lodge, which had been given to her as a wedding present, had been returned to the Kenyan people when the country gained its independence in 1963. This was her first visit to Kenya since the four-hour stop over when I photographed her in 1972. Jomo Kenyatta had since died and she took the opportunity to visit his grave. She also spent Armistice Day there and went to the Nairobi war cemetery where 2,000 African dead are buried. The order of service was familiar, with *O God Our Help in Ages Past*, Binyon's poem *For the Fallen* and two minutes silence. Silence is a mark of respect in Kenya so, although on her arrival half a million people lined the twelve-mile route from Jomo Kenyatta Airport to the city, when she first arrived they maintained a strict hush as she went past.

Opposite: In a prettily coloured ceremony India's Prime Minister Mrs Indira Gandhi welcomed the Queen and the Duke of Edinburgh to the presidential palace of Rashtrapati Bhavan in New Delhi on the last stage of their Commonwealth tour in November 1983. The Sikh Guards stand ominously in the background. Indira Gandhi was murdered by assassins from among those very guards less than a year later. The Queen then sent a message of condolence to Rajiv Gandhi, her son and successor. 'The world and the Commonwealth have lost one of their most distinguished leaders,' she said. Less than eight years later, in May 1991, Rajiv was himself murdered in an appalling bomb attack, and the Queen, once again, sent a message, this time to the President of India, expressing her sadness at the death of such a staunch supporter of the Commonwealth.

The Queen visited Bangladesh in November 1983. The evening light catches this group at a garden party in the presidential palace at Bangabhaban. The Queen is walking with the Administrator of Dhaka, Major-General Mahmudul Hassan as flower girls scatter petals at her feet. This was her first visit to Bangladesh since the country split from Pakistan. When she arrived she was greeted by President Chowdhury and by Lieutenant-General Ershad, the Chief Martial Law Administrator, but the ceremonial welcome was postponed to the following morning. Then, after laying a wreath and planting a tree at the national war memorial, the Queen and the Duke of Edinburgh drove to the presidential palace. The parade of honour there was led by the Bengal Lancers in red tunics, white breeches, and blue-crested headgear, carrying flags and looking impressively ferocious.

On 25th October 1984 the Queen attended a banquet given by French President François Mitterand at the French Ambassador's residence in London. The Queen speaks fluent French, of course, and she often visits that country in a private capacity. She is known as Duke of Normandy by some of her subjects: the Channel Islands are a British dependent territory but also part of the Duchy of Normandy. Although the French sovereign took over that title in the thirteenth century, the Queen is still referred to as Duke by the islanders.

Opposite: The Queen watches field trials in 1985 away from the cares of state. In her Christmas message that year these seemed at first to weigh heavy. 'Looking at the morning newspapers, listening to the radio and watching the television, it is only too easy to conclude that nothing is going right in the world', she said. 'All this year we seem to have had nothing but bad news with a constant stream of reports of 'plane crashes, earthquakes, volcanic eruptions and famine – and as if natural disasters were not enough, we hear of riots, wars, acts or terrorism and generally of man's inhumanity to man. It used to be said that "no news is good news" but today you might well think that "good news is no news".' But she went on to talk of the 'quiet courage and dedication' of the many people she meets each year who come to Buckingham Palace to be honoured for saving lives. 'There is a lot of good news and some wonderful things are going on in spite of the frightening headlines,' she said.

Members of the royal family and Buckingham Palace staff wave goodbye as the newly married Duke and Duchess of York leave for their honeymoon after their wedding on 23rd July 1986. It was a momentous day, and the previous night on television the bride had said that above all she wanted everyone to enjoy themselves. I was able to enjoy the party, as the Duke had asked his friend and mentor, Gene Nocon, to supervise the wedding photography. Gene chose Albert Watson, the New York based fashion photographer to take the official pictures, and he also persuaded over a hundred of his photographer colleagues to take a photograph of whatever they were doing that day. The resulting pictures were mounted in an album and presented to the Duke and Duchess. The idea was later adapted for the famous book *One Day for Life*.

Opposite: Karsh's study of the Queen, wearing Canadian orders, and the Duke of Edinburgh was one of a series taken for the Canadian Government during her tour of Canada in late September 1984, postponed from July because of the Canadian general election. She said at the end of it to a gathering of United Empire Loyalists, 'The crowds of people of all ethnic origins and denominations who gave me such a warm welcome demonstrated that the Crown still has a real value, and I shall continue to fulfil my duties as Queen of Canada to the best of my abilities and in the interest of all Canadians.'

Children from all over the Commonwealth gathered in front of Buckingham Palace to give the Queen daffodils on her sixtieth birthday. This is one of my favourite pictures of all. With the compressed line of youth balanced by the Queen it is a demonstration of how the telephoto lens can, by contracting the scene, add so much. The feeling it gives reminds me of the story of Sir Walter Raleigh's cape. The children had all just marched down The Mall carrying a daffodil each, and after they had belted out a birthday song the Queen went down to meet them. On the Queen's left is Neville Labovitch who organised the event, the late Victor Chapman who imbued the press office with the spirit of Canada, and Lieutenant-Colonel Blair Stewart-Wilson, Deputy Master of the Household.

Opposite: The Queen exchanges words with a young girl in Great Yarmouth on 1st August 1985. I like the communication which is obviously taking place. The girl is not overawed by the occasion, and the Queen is in no sense patronising the younger generation. It is quite remarkable how children feel at ease in the Queen's presence and very often they prick the pomposity of formal occasion when civic dignitaries are standing around nervously hoping that nothing will go wrong.

Karsh captures the Queen and the Duke of Edinburgh posing with their grandchildren, Princes William and Harry, Peter and Zara Phillips, at Balmoral in 1987. It is Karsh at his best with the royal family. He has considerable charm and has coaxed genuine smiles from the children, which is not easy. This study was used for the Queen and Prince Philip's personal Christmas card in 1987. The Queen had said in her previous Christmas message: 'The happy arrival of our fourth grandchild gave great cause for family celebrations. But for parents and grandparents a birth is also time for reflection on what the future holds for the baby and how they can best ensure its safety and happiness. To do that, I believe we must be prepared to learn as much from them as they do from us.'

Opposite: The Queen and the Duke of Edinburgh are pictured on the occasion of the Queen's 60th birthday, taken by their son Prince Andrew. This reminds me so much of iconographic paintings of American frontiersmen and their wives. Prince Philip ought to be holding a pitchfork! The printer Gene Nocon is the Prince's photographic guru and his influence is evident here. His book, *Photographic Printing*, set the pace on the subject, and he has been printer for many of the most famous photgraphers. He came into the public eye in 1986 when he picked up a camera to take the engagement picture, of Prince Andrew and Sarah Ferguson, which was used on the commemorative stamp. He became deeply involved as photographic adviser to their wedding, and was actually on the balcony of Buckingham Palace, with his camera, crawling out of sight beneath the Duke and Duchess of York as they kissed in front of the nation.

This is a lovely picture of the Queen and Princess
Margaret at the Chelsea Flower Show on 20th May
1985. After music and ballet, gardening is Princess
Margaret's great joy and she always attends this event.
It has been held in the grounds of the Royal Hospital at
Chelsea since 1913 by the Royal Horticultural Society.
In its early days it was helped rather than hindered by
the Great War. It was seen as useful to foster the
cultivation of fruit and vegetables amongst the masses.
A report of the show in 1915 in *The Gentlewoman* said at
the time: 'Chelsea Flower Show is not a gala; there is no
merrymaking or essence of the carnival, all of which in
these times would be most offensive to the English
mind, plunged as it is in so much sadness. It is purely a
year's record of horticultural enterprise.' Nowadays over
200,000 people go each year, turning the Royal Hospital
into a sea of muddy grass and umbrellas, and making
Chelsea impossible to drive through for about a week.

In what has become a popular tradition, Queen Elizabeth the Queen Mother came out of Clarence House to acknowledge crowds on her 86th birthday on 4th August 1986, just over a week after the wedding of the Duke and Duchess of York. All through Queen Elizabeth's life she has received tributes from those around her. Lady Airlie said the young Lady Elizabeth was 'very unlike the cocktail drinking, chain-smoking girls who came to be regarded as typical of the 1920s. Her radiant vitality and a blend of gaiety, kindness and sincerity made her irresistible to men.' She had so many admirers that when her engagement to the Duke of York was announced, politician and bon viveur Chips Channon remarked that 'the clubs are in gloom'. She became a model member of the royal family. *The Times* noted that she 'lays a foundation stone as though she had just discovered a new and delightful way of spending an afternoon'. Hitler called her: 'The most dangerous woman in Europe'. Her lifelong friend Lord David Cecil once said: 'Her sense of duty and patriotism

are helped by her dramatic sense. She thinks she *ought* to wave and give pleasure. And she is able to perform these feelings to the public.' Her grandson Prince Charles wrote of her, 'She belongs to that priceless brand of human beings whose greatest gift is to enhance life for others through her own effervescent enthusiasm for life.' The royal family are, from left to right: The Duke and Duchess of York, the Queen, the Prince and Princess of Wales, Queen Elizabeth, Viscount Linley and his mother Princess Margaret.

In 1986, for only the second time in the history of the
two countries, the King and Queen of Spain visited
Britain; yet relations go back to 1254 when Prince
Edward travelled to Castile to marry Princess Eleanora.
The Spanish monarchy, which was restored in 1975, has
always maintained close connections with Britain. King
Juan Carlos and Queen Sofia often paid private visits to
Broadlands in Hampshire to stay with the King's cousin
Lord Mountbatten, and first Prince Charles and his
family, and now the Queen and the Duke of Edinburgh
have been to stay with their Spanish cousins on holiday
at the Marivent Summer Palace on Majorca. The Queen
paid a state visit to Spain in 1988, the year of the 400th
anniversary of the Spanish Armada. Now that Spain has
joined the European Community and problems over
Gibraltar have eased there are even better links between
the countries.

At the Queen's Birthday Parade, the Trooping the Colour, in June 1987, the Queen was driven for the first time in an open carriage. The horse she normally rode, Burmese retired in 1987 aged 25. The appearance of the Queen in the ivory phaeton wearing a summer frock was not universally popular. Some people felt it lacked the majesty of former years when the Queen paraded on horseback dressed in the uniform of the regiment whose colour was to be trooped (see right). The official reason for the change was the difficulty of training another horse to the same standard – praise indeed for Burmese. That horse had been given to the Queen by the Canadian Government from the stables of the Royal Canadian Mounted Police. He used to prick up its ears to the sound of the tune *Colonel Bogey*. After three years of retirement sadly he died at Windsor in 1990.

After polo on Smith's Lawn near Windsor on 28th July 1985, the Queen congratulates the captain of the winning team. Through hard work the Prince of Wales, has become a respected figure. He never tries to avoid the unceasing responsibilities which come with his title and is far from being a passive force in the large number of successful organizations and dynamic charities with which he is involved. His work is designed to encourage and promote the well-being of people everywhere. He undertakes 200 public engagements per year, as many as six a day, with several foreign tours. He has to plan his schedule a year in advance from his offices in Buckingham Palace, with the help of three private secretaries, a press secretary and a number of equerries. It ranges from tours of factories and areas of high unemployment, through to conservation and protection of the environment. He cares passionately about the preservation of Britain's natural beauty, the reduction of pollution, and fights long battles against unsightly architecture. He has even clashed with the government over subjects like acid rain. He wants, one day, to be a monarch who knows the needs of his subjects.

The Duchess of Windsor died on 24th April 1986, over
fifty years after her liason with King Edward VIII began
at his home Fort Belvedere. By 1986 the Duchess had
been a widow, living in Paris for nearly fifteen years.
Her lily-covered oak coffin was flown to RAF Benson
where it was met by the Duke of Gloucester who
accompanied it to Windsor. On 29th April it left St
George's Chapel after the funeral service on the
shoulders of eight Welsh guardsmen, to be buried beside
her husband at Frogmore. Those who attended the
service as well as the Queen, the Duke of Edinburgh,
Queen Elizabeth the Queen Mother, the Prince and
Princess of Wales, and the Princess Royal, included
friends of the Duchess such as Lady Alexandra Metcalfe
and Grace, Countess of Dudley.

The highlight of the Princess Royal's racing life was the
Dresden Diamond Stakes Ladies Race at Ascot on 25th
July 1987 which she won on Ten No Trumps. It is a
passion she has developed from her three-day eventing
and which she inherits from the Queen. 'I've always
wanted to have success,' she has said. 'I enjoy the
business of riding out and going to the races, and to
have a winner certainly makes a difference to the level of
enjoyment.' Mark Phillips expressed concern about her
racing. 'Yes I do worry,' he said. 'But not because of the
way *she* rides, but because of all the others in the race.
It's not always what you do in racing, it's what the other
jockeys do or don't do that causes the trouble.' Princess
Anne was honoured in her mother's birthday honours in
1986 with the title Princess Royal, formerly held by
King George V's daughter Princess Mary, Countess of
Harewood.

The Queen talks to Maoris in Auckland, New Zealand, in February 1986. Although these Maoris are friendly her tour was dogged by protests about their land-rights. The Treaty of Waitangi under which they ceded New Zealand to Queen Victoria in return for traditional lands and fisheries was never ratified so has been ignored. At one point an egg was thrown at the Queen and hit her pink coat. 'We're bloody protesting, that's what!' yelled one of the egg-chuckers while being dragged away by police. 'The Queen's come here and they aren't honouring the treaty!' New Zealand Prime Minister David Lange apologized to the Queen about the incident, but she took it in good part. At a banquet she said, sportingly, 'New Zealand has long been renowned for its dairy products, though I myself prefer New Zealand eggs for breakfast'. The Queen's Speech, which she read later at New Zealand's Parliament, underlined the government's pro-Maori policies and mentioned forthcoming legislation recognizing Maori as an official language.

At Devonport on 21st July 1988, the same year that she visited Spain, the Queen was amused as the Duke of Edinburgh added a stitch to a giant Armada tapestry, watched by its owners Tom Mor and Dorothy Cull. That evening the Queen and the Duke attended an Armada dinner on the shore-based *HMS Drake* at Devonport commemorating the victory over the Spanish of 1588. She had just arrived at Plymouth on board *Britannia* from another anniversary. The day before she had been to Torbay as part of the tercentenary of the Glorious Revolution, when William and Mary came to Britain. The Queen was joined by Prince Willem Alexander, the twenty-one year old heir to the Dutch throne. Earlier that year she had been the guest of Queen Beatrix in Holland where the two of them saw the William and Mary exhibition at the Nieuwe Kerk, accompanied by their consorts Prince Klaus and the Duke of Edinburgh.

Opposite: The Queen and Queen Elizabeth the Queen Mother study the form of runners at the Epsom Derby, the only English classic the Queen has never won, on 1st June 1988. It is a great picture showing their shared interest. The Derby was started by the 12th Earl of Derby in 1780. The present peer, the 18th, is extremely keen on racing, as was his father. The 17th Earl of Derby who died in 1948 was a friend of King George V. He was also a noted politician, though Field Marshal Haig said he was 'a very weak-minded fellow, and, like the feather pillow, bears the marks of the last person who has sat on him'. As a racing man, though, he was indomitable. He brought bloodlines to the fore which are still cherished by owners today. In a long career his stable won stake money of roughly £845,000 over 1,000 races. He won his ancestor's race no less than three times. He was flamboyant too. One of his favourite animals fell ill and he had it put at once on a diet of three dozen eggs, and a bottle each of port and brandy per day. History does not relate whether it survived.

On 12th October 1986 the Queen and the Duke of
Edinburgh landed at Peking airport for a historic
nine-day, 3,000-mile tour of China and Hong Kong.
Historic, because this was the first time a British
monarch had ever been to China, home to a quarter of
the world's population. On the third day she met the
chairman of the Communist Party, leader of one billion
people, Deng Xiaoping, aged 82 and a heavy smoker,
but younger, the Queen pointed out, than her mother.
This was the man who was pushing China's
modernisation programme. He had survived a turbulent
political career, purged in 1966, rehabilitated in 1973,
pushed out again in 1976, and back again in 1977, but
was still overwhelmed by the Queen. 'Thank you for
coming to see such an old man as me,' he told her when
they met. That afternoon, after lunch with this political
titan, came one of the Queen's most eagerly anticipated
visits: to the Great Wall of China, pictured here. She
left her staff and half the camera crews of the civilized
world panting as she marched for a quarter of a mile up
a steep incline to get a good view. Even the Duke of
Edinburgh was glowing slightly. She then announced to
the exhausted journalists that she would like her picture
taken, 'so that I can prove I'm here'.

The one year-old Princess Beatrice, her grandmother
the Queen, and parents the Duke and Duchess of York
set sail for their holiday in Balmoral in August 1989.
This is a journey which begins annually for the Royal
Yacht *Britannia* on the Solent during Cowes Week. She
cruises up Britain's west coast to Scotland's Western
Isles, and then on to call in on Scrabster harbour to visit
Queen Elizabeth the Queen Mother at the Castle of
Mey. The ritual there never varies. It is always at
11 a.m. and they are always met off the royal barge by
Queen Elizabeth. When they leave for Aberdeen, the
nearest port to Balmoral, Queen Elizabeth fires rockets
from the battlements of Mey and in return the Queen
shoots flares from *Britannia*. Arrival at Aberdeen is
usually at 6 a.m. so, to preserve peace for the Queen to
sleep, the engines are cut to Silent Order. Builders
working nearby have been asked to take a tea break to
keep the noise down.

The Maundy Service, which dates from the 12th century, marks the day when Christ washed the feet of his disciples. The tradition of the monarch washing the feet of a selection of subjects was stopped in 1730, but alms are still distributed to the poor. In the right hand foreground of this picture, taken at Exeter Cathedral, is Regimental Sergeant-Major Phillips who used to scream at me at the Royal Military Academy at Sandhurst while I was on my way to the Grenadier Guards. He is a Welsh Guardsman who went on to run St James's Palace. When I first knew him he was a college RSM under Sergeant-Major Lord, the Academy RSM who shrivelled our ears with the news that 'He's the Lord up there and I'm the Lord down here stand up STRAIGHT!'. Their job was to make the lives of officer cadets a misery in an effort to shape the British army into the world's supreme fighting force. We called them 'sir' and they called us 'sir', and we were the ones who meant it. 'Stand still you idle little monarch' – was one particularly explosive command I remember. It was directed at King Hussein of Jordan.

This is a quintessentially English picture. It says village
life, bees and lawn-mowers and 'If Wet In The
Vicarage' in equal quantities. In fact it is a garden party
held at Buckingham Palace for the Not Forgotten
Association of war veterans. This is one of the smaller
garden parties that every summer bring guests across the
Palace's famous camomile lawn. There are three large
parties, every year, to which a total of 30,000 people are
invited. They always start at 3.15 p.m. and the Queen
appears exactly at 4 o'clock. The bands play, the guests
sip their tea in striped pavilions and those who are
particularly fortunate have a chance to talk to the Queen
or other members of the royal family.

In May 1991 the Queen paid her third state visit to the United States of America. She presented President Bush with the Winston Churchill Commemorative Medal at a ceremony on the White House lawn and the world's pressmen were there to record every second. Of the hundreds of photographs taken, I particularly like the one above, because it captures a moment of spontaneity, unrehearsed and therefore more relaxed. The same applies to the picture of the Queen with Mrs Bush at the Marshall Heights Leisure Centre, a community centre in a deprived area, known locally as Dodge City. Throughout this book these are the pictures I have tended to select, because they are the ones that best convey the Queen's warm personality contained within such dignity and grace.

Acknowledgements In a book of this nature a number of people have to remain uncredited, but the author would like to thank the staff of the Australian High Commission, Liz Belton, the Press Office at Buckingham Palace, the Canadian High Commission, Dharani Rethnam of the Commonwealth Secretariat, Penny Daly, Mike Ersser, the Fiji Embassy, the Office of the Duke and Duchess of Gloucester, Paul Grant, Anwar and Caroline Hussein, the High Commissioner for India, the Jamaican High Commission, Peter Kain, the Kenya High Commission, Elizabeth Kerr, the Malta High Commission, the staff at Martini & Rossi, the High Commissioner for New Zealand, the Nigeria High Commission, the staff at the Royal Photographic Society, the Tonga High Commission, the office of the Prince and Princess of Wales, Paul Watkins, Roger Wemyss-Brooks, and the Chancery of the Archdiocese of Westminster.

The author is also extremely grateful for help from the following who supplied pictures: Godfrey Argent, Associated Press, Baron Studios, Robert Beer, Ronald Bell, BBC, Camera Press, Government of Canada, Central Office of Information, CPNA Pool, John Downing, Kent Gavin, Tim Graham, James Gray, Robin Gray, Steve Hartley, The Hulton Picture Company, Anwar Hussein, Margaret Lavender, Mike Maloney, Anthony Marshall, Ministry of Defence, Brendan Monks, Bernard Parkin, Press Association, Press Photo Combine, Mike Roberts, Royal Archives, John Shelley, Sothebys, Sport & General Press Agency, Tom Stoddart, Syndication International, The Times, Universal Pictorial Press, Philip Way.